Nothing to Declare

ANN MURPHY is a senior news reporter with the *Evening Echo* in Cork. She is the newspaper's security correspondent and has worked on major crime stories in the southern area, including the biggest cocaine seizure in the history of the State, off the coast of West Cork in 2007. She won the Justice Media Award for regional newspapers in 2006. Before working with the *Evening Echo*, Ann was a senior news reporter with *Inside Cork*. She also worked with Leader Group Newspapers in Ballincollig.

NOTHING
TO DECLARE

The drug smugglers' deadly trade

Ann Murphy

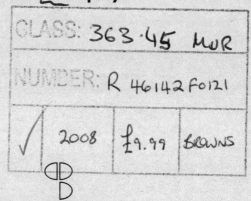
THE O'BRIEN PRESS
DUBLIN

First published 2008 by The O'Brien Press Ltd,
12 Terenure Road East, Rathgar, Dublin 6, Ireland.
Tel: +353 1 4923333; Fax: +353 1 4922777
E-mail: books@obrien.ie
Website: www.obrien.ie

ISBN: 978-1-84717-106-1

Photographs are copyright to the following:
Courtesy of Revenue Commissioners; Paddy O'Sullivan; the *Evening Echo/Irish Examiner;*
Eugene O'Sullivan; Richard Mills/*Evening Echo;* Asset Forfeiture Unit, South Africa.

British Library Cataloguing-in-Publication Data
A catalogue record for this title is available from the British Library

1 2 3 4 5 6 7 8 9 10
08 09 10 11 12 13 14 15

Layout and design: The O'Brien Press Ltd.
Printed and bound in the UK by J.H. Haynes & Co Ltd, Sparkford

Dedication

For my beloved family, and for families damaged by drug
addiction.

Acknowledgements

Without the contributions of many interviewees, *Nothing to Declare* would not have come to fruition. Among them are several serving and retired members of An Garda Síochána, customs and the navy, who gave me a better understanding of their roles in drugs law enforcement in Ireland.

The assistance of the staff of the navy, Revenue, Gardaí, the Irish Prison Service and the Courts Service was invaluable, including their press offices. Thanks also to those in similar agencies in Northern Ireland, the UK, the United States and South Africa.

The contribution of people working at the coalface with drug addicts was an eye-opener but nothing could have prepared me for the story of one addict, who was kind enough to share his experiences with me. A special thanks to you, Liam.

The expertise and patience of the staff in the library of the *Evening Echo/Irish Examiner*, and Cork City Library were extremely valuable. So too was the legal advice from Darryl Broderick and Adrian Wall in Ronan Daly Jermyn.

Thanks too to Síle, Mark, Tom, Eileen and Edel for their constructive criticism, and to Colum Cronin for his keen eye.

Thanks to my media colleagues, particularly Ralph Riegel of the *Irish Independent*, who helped me through each stage of writing my first book. Thanks also to Philip Nolan of the *Irish Daily Mail*; Stephen Rogers and Liam Heylin of the *Irish Examiner*; and Nashira Davids of The *Sunday Times*, in South Africa, for their advice, and to Paul Byrne of TV3 for planting the seed in my head for this book.

The support of my colleagues in the *Evening Echo* is greatly appreciated, including editor Maurice Gubbins, chief executive Dan Linehan, news editors Emma Connolly, Elaine Duggan and Mary Smithwick, and my fellow reporters, including Ronan Bagnall and Mark Barry, who worked with me on the Dunlough Bay case. A special thanks to pictures editor Brian Lougheed for the efforts he put in to sourcing photographs.

Thanks too to the Revenue press office and Paddy O'Sullivan, and other sources in Ireland and South Africa for supplying other images.

I also want to acknowledge the support of the staff of the O'Brien Press Ltd, particularly Michael O'Brien, Síne Quinn, Mary Webb and Claire McVeigh.

Most importantly, *Nothing to Declare* would not have seen the light of day without the support of those closest to me. Heartfelt gratitude to Liam, Joan, Síle, John Joe and Susan, and extended family and friends.

CONTENTS

INTRODUCTION

The *Lucky Day* made its way across the Atlantic from Barbados, following a well-worn path towards Ireland and Europe. The ten-year-old vessel had stopped off in the Caribbean en route from Margarita, an island off Venezuela. Content with the progress of the mission, the three men on board were looking ahead to off-loading their cargo close to the south coast of Ireland in four weeks' time. Unbeknownst to them, the cargo would be the largest ever seizure of cocaine by Irish law enforcement agencies.

* * *

When it arrived close to Ireland in July 2007, the *Lucky Day* was one of thousands of vessels that have made the journey from the tip of South America with drug cargos for the cocaine users of Western Europe within the past two decades. Europe is the second largest cocaine market in the world, behind the US. Law enforcers across Europe fight a daily battle to stem the illegal drugs trade – as the Colombian cartels controlling the industry continue to make billions of dollars. Traditional international cocaine smuggling routes start in South America, in countries including Colombia, Venezuela and Peru. Smugglers travelling by sea come east towards Europe, aided by the warm fast-flowing currents of the Gulf Stream, which run close to Ireland's southwest coast. They then head to Spain, Portugal, the Netherlands or northwest Africa, from which points the gangs dispatch their wares to Ireland, the UK and other parts of Europe. The abandoning of traditional routes across the Caribbean in favour of new routes through West African countries, like Guinea Bissau and Senegal, to other parts of the world was signalled in the 2007 report of the United Nations Office on Drugs and Crime (UNODC).

However, the drug barons of South America are not alone in controlling the world drug trade. In the east, supplies of heroin are being transported across the world from the opium-producing Afghanistan, while cannabis is being pumped into Europe from Morocco. The increase in opium production in Afghanistan was identified as another significant development in 2007 by UNODC. The Afghans control more than 90 per cent of the world's opium production.

When the cocaine cargo aboard the *Lucky Day* was transferred to a smaller rib, off the coast of Ireland in the early hours of 2 July 2007, the barons behind the shipment were dealt a savage blow when the treacherous seas cost them millions of euro by overturning the rib carrying the consignment. It resulted in the Joint Drugs Taskforce involving the Gardaí, navy and customs seizing 1,550kg from the sea, initially valued at €107 million. In its annual report for 2007, the Irish Revenue Commissioners revealed that the agency had been involved in the seizure of almost €139 million worth of illegal drugs that year. The overall figure was inflated by the value of the Dunlough Bay seizure, which later grew to be worth €440 million – once analysis of the haul revealed it to be 75 per cent pure.

Until then, Ireland's most significant seizure of cocaine was made in Cobh in 1996, when a rummage on board a converted trawler named the *Sea Mist* recovered 599kg of the drug. It was one of three major seizures of drugs off vessels in Ireland that year. Such large-scale hauls were a wake-up call to law enforcers during that period. The attempt to smuggle an arms shipment into Ireland, through Kerry, on board the *Marita Ann* in September 1984 had shown how the southwest coast has long been seen as a safe haven for smugglers. Now, the exploitation of Ireland's vast, rugged coastline by drug traffickers was obvious and it had to be addressed. The Coastal Watch programme was set up and involved the sharing of intelligence between Gardaí, customs and excise, the navy, residents and maritime workers in coastal areas. A memorandum of understanding was also drawn up between Gardaí, customs and the navy to develop closer links in policing the coast.

The 1996 seizures came amid a major crackdown on organised and drug-related crime, prompted by the murders of crime journalist Veronica Guerin and Detective Garda Jerry McCabe, within weeks of each other that year. The establishment of the Criminal Assets Bureau (CAB) later in the year to target the assets gained by criminals through their illegal activities was seen as a major success. It prompted many of Ireland's significant drug dealers to move to Continental Europe to escape the rigours of the new agency. However, it is suspected that some of these figures still pull the strings in landing some consignments of illegal drugs on Irish soil – without handling the drugs themselves.

There is also evidence to suggest that vessels come to Ireland, en route to elsewhere to deliver or collect drugs. In one case, customs officers boarded a suspect fishing vessel in Ballycotton to search it. Although they found nothing, the officers took details of the Dutch crew members, and discovered, through enquiries, that they had links to a criminal in their homeland, who also arrived in Ireland some time later. The information was passed to the Dutch authorities and surveillance was placed on the vessel, which was subsequently apprehended after it had collected cannabis in Morocco. In another case, six tonnes of cocaine was found on board a vessel called the *MV Limerick* which ran aground off Guantanamo in October 1996. The vessel had been purchased in Ireland and was previously known as the *Angelus*. Information about the vessel had been passed on by Irish customs to their counterparts in the UK and the US, after they became suspicious when a Colombian arrived in Ireland to buy it. Its progress towards South America was trailed by US customs, who notified Cuban authorities when it reached Guantanamo. When they raided the vessel in one of the few joint collaborations between the two countries, the cocaine was found hidden in parts of the vessel.

The Dunlough Bay seizure was used by customs officers to point out the need for further investment to help them police Irish shores. At the time of the seizure, the agency had just one cutter boat, *An Suirbhéir*, to serve the entire country's coastline. An announcement was made in February 2008 that a second such vessel was being commissioned with the same remit. The announcement also included plans for a new scanner to detect drugs and cigarettes being smuggled in through ferry ports on containers. Both were due to be in operation in 2009.

On an international level, an EU taskforce, involving Ireland, Britain, the Netherlands, France, Spain, Portugal and Italy, was launched in September 2007, to tackle drug trafficking in the region. The taskforce, known as the Maritime Analysis and Operation Centre-Narcotics (MAOC-N), is based in Lisbon, in Portugal, and aims to improve international co-operation against drug trafficking. Final preparations for the setting up of the task-force were being made, when the Dunlough Bay discovery was made. Ireland's then Minister for Justice, Brian Lenihan, attended the launch of the new centre in Lisbon. Speaking there, he pointed out that 16 per cent of European waters are in the Irish zone. He added: 'The reasons for Irish participation in this initiative are obvious. The pooling of resources will lead to vastly increased monitoring of suspicious vessels heading towards Irish waters.'

The fight to stem the supply of drugs in Ireland does not come cheap. Investigations into coastal drug seizures involve several hundreds of hours of manpower. The cost to the State when proceedings reach the court stage is also immeasurable, according to the Courts Service. Referring to the two sets of court proceedings it took to convict three men in connection with a significant cannabis seizure, near the Fastnet Rock, in 1999, Freedom of Information Officer with the Courts Service, Miriam O'Flanagan, said: 'In order to establish the full cost to the State of these two proceedings, it would be necessary to include the time of the solicitors, barristers, Gardaí, customs officials, navy officers, forensic scientists, court staff and the Judge involved in the case and should also include an overhead charge for the use of the (court) building. The overall cost is therefore virtually impossible to calculate as it is difficult to identify the number of hours involved in bringing this case to prosecution and the hourly cost for each grade within each group involved.'

While the cost to the State of such cases is indeterminate, some recompense has been gained in the past two decades, through the sale of vessels detained in operations involving maritime drug seizures. For example, Revenue earned £108,211.53 through the sale of the *Sea Mist*, *Gemeos* and *Plongeur Wisky* vessels, seized in separate operations between 1996 and 1999.

Cases outlined in this book show the lengths to which international gangs will go to import drugs into countries like

Ireland. However, the coast is not the only gateway for drug barons. Another avenue exploited by major networks are the ports and airports of countries throughout the world. In April 2008 one of the largest cannabis seizures of recent years was made when a search of a container coming through Rosslare port was carried out by customs officers. More than 1,100kg of the drug was discovered in two pallets in the container, which had been marked as footwear. It proved that although cocaine use is rapidly growing in Ireland, cannabis remains the most popular illegal substance.

As this book shows, much ingenuity is used by drug smugglers to ensure their wares are not detected coming through customs areas of ports and airports. *Nothing to Declare* reveals how people are tempted into becoming couriers in the drug trafficking industry – ending up languishing in prisons thousands of kilometres from home.

It highlights some of the many high-profile attempts made to smuggle drugs into Ireland, through the south and west coasts in the past two decades. It examines how the 2007 seizure made its way into the waters off West Cork from the *Lucky Day*, and led to a money trail from there to South Africa. It remembers the *Posidonia* case in 1999, and the arrival of the *Sea Mist* into Cork harbour in September 1996, with 599kg of cocaine on board. The difficulties that forced the vessel into Cork harbour led to the downfall, eleven years later, of one of Europe's largest drug traffickers, Brian Wright. The stories of other individuals, such as Briton David Huck, Antrim businessman Colin Lees and Cork antiques dealer Christopher O'Connell are laid out here.

Nothing to Declare also looks at a case where Corkman, John O'Shea, pleaded guilty to being involved in a conspiracy to import drugs into Ireland, after the detention of a coaster in Castletownbere, which had been on its way to County Donegal. Despite an intricate search by Gardaí and customs officers, no trace of drugs was found on board. The role of Castletownbere in a more controversial discovery of cannabis resin in Urlingford, a year earlier, is included too.

The story of Irishman John O'Toole is also examined. As he awaited trial in Ireland after the seizure of cocaine on the *Gemeos* yacht in Kinsale, his wife died from cancer in Panama. During his trial, it was heard that he became involved in the *Gemeos* operation to raise money for treatment for his wife.

While drug barons in South America revel in their riches from the illicit trade, families throughout Ireland and other parts of Europe are torn apart by the damage wreaked by addiction to drugs, like cocaine. This book reveals how addiction drove one teenager away from his family and into a life of drug dealing. It looks at the spiralling number of deaths due to cocaine use in 2006 and 2007, and gets the opinions of people working at the coalface with addicts.

Nothing to Declare proves that drug trafficking leads to riches for few and heartache for many.

MULES

The drugs industry is viewed in some quarters as exciting, with huge profits to be made. Although the perception of a glamorous image may be true for the major players in the industry, drug smuggling can have a destructive impact on the lives of countless drug users and their families. However, the industry can also have deadly repercussions for smaller cogs in the drug smuggling trade – the mules. Each year, hundreds of people in poverty in countries like Ghana, Jamaica and South Africa are tempted to carry drugs in their luggage or hidden in their bodies to make money to pull themselves out of their financial problems.

Tonnette Andu was one such person. As she arrived into Cork airport from Nigeria, she was scared but she was also excited. She had travelled a long way, on her way to the United States. As she waited to go through customs in Cork airport's new terminal, she was looking forward to a better life in Chicago, which she had left fourteen years earlier at the tender age of six. Andu had been sent to live with her grandmother in Nigeria. She had never forgotten her first home in Chicago and the draw to the land of her birth was too strong to ignore.

However, Andu could not fly thousands of kilometres from Nigeria on a small budget. She worked as a teacher's aid in her grandmother's school in Nigeria. She also worked as a bus monitor. However, she did not have enough money to pay the fare from Lagos, the capital of Nigeria, to the United States. She later told Gardaí she also wanted money to help out her sister and her friend. In a statement made on the evening of her arrest, she said: 'My friend has nowhere to live, and my sister is pregnant and needs money to look after the baby.' Her sister lived in Chicago, while her friend was in Nigeria. When she was presented with an opportunity to earn extra money for her ticket through drug trafficking, she took it. This opportunity came with a price, and an element of fear. Andu was also not sure how much she would earn for carrying out this risky mission.

She became involved in the operation after meeting a man at a club in Lagos. Through him, she became acquainted with three other men, who were also involved in smuggling. Her new associates asked her to smuggle cocaine into Ireland. They wanted her to become a drugs courier, commonly known as a mule – someone who would carry drugs from one country to another by ferry or air. Andu was asked to swallow a quantity of cocaine, which she was later expected to pass through her system and give to someone waiting in Cork city. She was very apprehensive about the task, knowing that she could get caught with the drugs while going through airports en route to Cork. She was also concerned about the option of hiding capsules of cocaine in her body until she arrived in Cork. She was afraid that the capsules would explode inside her body during the flight.

However, after much thought, in September 2006 Andu agreed to act as a mule. She told Gardaí she had known the men for two months by then. She opted for the other option given to her – carrying nearly a kilo of cocaine concealed in her hair. A room was booked for her in a hotel in Cork, where she was to hand over the drugs to a man she had never met. Andu was given a mobile phone number to call when she arrived in the city.

Andu had plenty of time to think about the trip ahead and the risks associated with it, while the cocaine was being stitched into her hair. Despite her fears however, she went ahead with her task as planned. Before embarking on a flight to Amsterdam, she went to a hotel room in Lagos to collect the valuable cargo. She spent several hours in the room while extensions were added to her hair. Cotton bags containing plastic packages of cocaine were then stitched into the hair, which was shaped into a beehive style to conceal them. When the job was complete, 888gm of the drug had been secured into place. The next step was to board the flight for Holland, hoping she would get through customs checks there before travelling to Cork. She was to spend two days in Cork before catching a flight to New York, from where she would travel to Chicago.

Andu breathed a sigh of relief when she managed to get as far as Cork without being detected. However, it was in Cork airport's customs area her dreams of a new life in America were shattered. A customs officer became suspicious of Andu's hairstyle, because the officer had seen similar attempts to conceal drugs on training videos. Andu was searched and the intricate measures to hide the drugs on behalf of the traffickers were laid bare. The drugs were cut out of her hair and she was arrested and taken to the nearby Garda station in Togher. During an interview in the station, Gardaí asked if she was going to smuggle drugs anywhere else other than Cork. She replied: 'No, I was told to come directly here.' She said the men who had involved her in the trafficking plot had guaranteed her safety. She told Gardaí that she planned to buy her ticket to the US in Ireland.

When the drugs were analysed, the haul was found to be worth more than €62,200, meaning that her crime fell under the most serious category of drugs possession. In Ireland, there are three levels of drug possession – simple possession, possession for sale or supply, and possession of more than €13,000 for sale or supply. The latter carries a mandatory sentence of ten years in prison, under Section 15A of the Misuse of Drugs Act 1977. Andu was charged with the most serious offence. When the case came before Judge Seán Ó Donnabháin for sentencing, Andu was given a prison sentence of three years. The judge said he was taking her circumstances into account, along with her co-operation with Gardaí and her early guilty plea. Judge Ó Donnabháin had earlier heard from Sergeant Jason Lynch of the Cork City Garda Drugs Unit that Andu had supplied Gardaí with names of people in Nigeria, who had given her instructions on how to carry out the transaction. In handing down the sentence, Judge Ó Donnabháin ruled that the last eighteen months would be suspended on the grounds that she would leave Ireland after her release and not return for two years. A stamp was placed on her passport to ensure that authorities in Ireland would be able to prevent her entry if she attempted to return through ports or airports within the ban period. Andu served her sentence in Limerick prison and was released from there in November 2007.

Law enforcement officers feel that offers of high money regularly tempt mules back into drug smuggling. In a *Panorama* documentary screened on BBC2, in January 2008, Blur bassist Alex James travelled to Colombia to explore the cocaine industry. Colombian president Alvaro Uribe invited him to visit the country after Mr James said he had spent stg£1 million on cocaine and champagne use. During his exploration of the cocaine trade in Colombia, he met a drugs mule in a prison. The man, an American named Steve, was serving a sentence of two years and seven months for smuggling heroin and cocaine. He said he knew several people who had smuggled drugs ten or twelve times without getting caught by authorities. Steve told Alex James that he will get involved in smuggling again as soon as he is released from prison.

Tonnette Andu's case was remarkable for the unusual method used to import the cocaine into Ireland. However, Andu is one of hundreds of mules sent from Africa and South America every year to import drugs into Europe through airports and ferry ports. Thirty-five mules were apprehended in Dublin Airport in 2007, while a further six were detected attempting to come through Cork Airport.

The case of Dubliner Róisín Zoe Savage proves that Irish people can also be used as mules and be imprisoned abroad. The mother of two is currently on probation in Ecuador, after she was detected in Quito Airport in 2003 with a bag that had 2.5kg of cocaine hidden in its lining. The London-based mother was on her way home to her family after travelling to Ecuador to help an African friend, who had told her he had trouble getting a visa in the South American country. The Dubliner was jailed for eight years for drugs offences. She claimed the drugs were planted on her – by her friend – and her family launched a campaign in Ireland to have her repatriated to serve the remainder of her sentence in Ireland. Dublin-based TD, Pat Carey, who knew Savage when he was vice-principal of her school, gave his support to the campaign. Coincidentally, Carey became Minister with responsibility for Ireland's national drugs strategy in 2007. Hopes were high that she would be returned to Ireland in 2005, when Ecuador signed up to the Strasbourg Convention. The convention allows a prisoner to be repatriated, for either a pardon or completion of a prison sentence, if the prisoner and both countries involved consent to the move. However, Savage was instead released from prison and placed on probation in Ecuador until the eight-year sentence handed to her expires in 2012. Efforts to have her repatriated to Ireland were continuing in 2008.

Customs officers and immigration police in airports and ports throughout Europe are constantly targeting flights and ferries, with a view to making it financially unviable for drug traffickers to use mules to move cocaine and other drugs. In Holland, a special focus has been put on couriers from South America and the Caribbean by the Dutch customs agency. Since 2005, a 'hundred per cent control' of aircraft coming from the targeted areas has been underway, meaning that intensive checks are being carried out on passengers on flights from the two regions. According to the World Customs Organisation's (WCO) annual report for 2006, four or five couriers were typically found on each targeted flight when the programme got underway. The number has now decreased to an average of less than 0.5 couriers per flight. Dutch police and customs officers are also on duty at border controls in Bonaire and Curacao since mid-2005, checking passengers en route to Holland for drugs.

Despite the concentration on couriers from the Caribbean

and South America, traffickers are continuing to despatch couriers through Amsterdam to Ireland and other parts of Europe by using alternative routes. Cocaine trafficking into Western Europe from Africa is becoming increasingly evident, as demonstrated by the case of Tonnette Andu. This trend was highlighted in the World Customs Report 2006, which revealed Nigeria and Ghana as the main departure and transit countries for couriers smuggling the drug through Africa.

This comes as no surprise to a UK-based group called Hibiscus, which looks after the welfare of foreign inmates in British prisons. The organisation's director, Olga Heaven, says that African countries have taken over from Jamaica in recent years as favoured routes into Europe by drug traffickers. Routes are regularly changed by traffickers as law enforcement agencies identify and crack down on the traditional channels. Olga Heaven says that a large number of Jamaicans had trafficked drugs into the UK in recent years but these were beginning to be replaced by couriers from Nigeria and Ghana and other parts of the Caribbean, shortly after the start of the new millennium.

South Africans are also regularly apprehended when trying to import drugs through British and Irish points of entry. Gardaí in the Santry Drugs Unit question those intercepted at Dublin Airport. According to figures from the unit, eight South Africans were among the thirty-five mules arrested at

Dublin airport in 2007. Ireland was the next highest represented country, with five couriers among those detained in the airport. Other nationalities found with illegal substances included Dutch, Nigerians and Venezuelans.

Efforts were made by Hibiscus to reduce the number of people becoming drugs couriers in Jamaica, and later Ghana. The group launched campaigns in both countries, aimed at educating financially-vulnerable people about the dangers of becoming a drugs mule. A similar campaign was planned for Nigeria in 2008. Ms Heaven claims that a lot of people recruited as mules are vulnerable and are not aware of the possibility of long jail sentences, if they are caught attempting to smuggle drugs into a foreign country. She says the long sentences couriers get are not enough of a deterrent because most are unaware of these before they leave home. She argues that couriers need to be educated before they leave their own country, if the number of people becoming involved in drug trafficking as mules is to be reduced.

Couriers are usually given a small sum of money initially, with a promise of a couple of thousand euro in total when the job is completed. The typical payment is in the region of €2,000. If their attempt is foiled, they will not get the money they have been promised and they also face a lengthy jail sentence in a foreign country.

While couriers may not be aware of the heavy sentences facing them if they are caught, traffickers themselves are. As a result, they rarely put themselves through the dangers of carrying out the drugs run. When they do, they usually carry very small quantities of drugs, making detection difficult. They are accompanied by couriers who carry much bigger quantities, putting them at increased risk of being caught.

Catching the traffickers behind the couriers is very difficult for police organisations across the world. This is because mules have very little information about the people who get them involved in the trade. In most instances, they know nothing apart from the first name of the person who got them involved. Typically, couriers also have very little information about the person they are supposed to pass the drugs to when they arrive in their destination country. They usually just have a first name and a phone number to contact to let them know they have arrived.

Governor of Mountjoy Prison in Dublin, John Lonergan, says that poverty is the main reason why people are lured into such a world. People are helped out in times of need and are later asked to repay the debt by becoming a drugs courier. He says this is particularly evident in the Dóchas centre, the female prison facility adjoining Mountjoy, where women from parts of Africa, South America and Central America regularly serve sentences for botched drugs operations.

Olga Heaven agrees. She says more than 90 per cent of mules are not users but get enlisted because of poverty and dependence on people who had given them help in times of difficulty. Women in impoverished situations are the main targets for bosses of drug smuggling enterprises, who can see the difficult situation they are in. In some instances, couriers have been duped into drug trafficking by members of their own family. Ms Heaven elaborates: 'In some cases involving Jamaican couriers, even their friends and family members have been involved in recruiting them. Those relatives would be living abroad in Europe and would tell their people at home that they would organise for them to come over. They would then tell them a short time before they leave that they have to take drugs with them.'

Couriers who fear being detected with cocaine hidden in their bodies are told by traffickers that the drugs cannot be detected internally by X-ray. A Garda source says couriers believe the traffickers and agree to have X-rays when they are asked to have one by suspicious police or customs officers.

Gardaí have come across cases where mules sent to Ireland were targeted by traffickers in coffee shops and bars in cities in Africa and the Netherlands. The source says: 'In one case, a South African man was in a bar and got drunk. He was taken out of the bar to a house in Johannesburg, where he was given a bath, given a new suit of clothes and taken to an airport to be put on a flight. He was given a suitcase. When he arrived in Ireland, he did not know where he was.' A quantity of drugs was found in his luggage and he received a prison sentence for the smuggling attempt.

John Lonergan believes that many mules arriving in Ireland do not even know where it is on the world map. In some cases, they do not have any English. He says they are pawns in the drug smuggling game and pay a huge penalty for getting caught while the drug godfathers usually escape the rigours of the law.

The first point of contact for drugs couriers in ports and airports are customs officers, who know that these people are acting on the orders of someone who has a much bigger role to play in the smuggling attempt. One of the biggest challenges facing officers in airports is identifying passengers who have swallowed large quantities of cocaine pellets that have been vacuum-packed in plastic. In many cases, the pellets are dipped in oil to make it easier to swallow them. Brian Smyth of Customs Drugs Law Enforcement says officers have come across incidents where people have hidden up to a kilo of drugs inside their bodies. In practical terms, this means they would have had to swallow up to a hundred pellets of compressed cocaine. Tonnette Andu did not use this method because she was too afraid of what could happen to her. Her concerns were justified, as there have been cases where the pellets have broken or exploded, posing a huge health risk to couriers.

A nineteen-year-old Estonian national, Maksim Gorbov, died in the Mid-Western Regional Hospital in Limerick in December 2002 after he became ill on a flight between Peru and Amsterdam. The KLM flight was diverted to Shannon when he became unwell. He admitted to flight staff that he had swallowed drugs. Pure cocaine had leaked into his body from its plastic wrapping, making him seriously ill. Despite being rushed to hospital, efforts to save him failed and he died shortly after arriving there. He had managed to pass twenty-five capsules of the drug through his system and an X-ray examination revealed sixty-nine more in his body. An inquest into his death heard that he had died from acute cardio-respiratory failure caused by ingesting cocaine. A verdict of death by misadventure was returned by the jury.

Cocaine is not the only drug which mules swallow or stuff into their bodies in a bid to complete a drugs run. In 1993 Corkman Jerry Kelly died in Liverpool after condoms containing 300 ecstasy tablets ruptured in his rectum. The Cobh native became ill on a Ryanair flight between Stansted and Dublin, shortly after the flight had taken off. The flight was diverted to Liverpool where the man was taken immediately to a local hospital. By that point he had lost consciousness, and he died shortly afterwards.

The campaign run in Ghana in 2007 by Hibiscus highlighted the possibility of a drugs mule dying after ingesting large quantities of cocaine. It took the form of a film called *Maame Goes to London*. The film showed the death of a drugs courier after a pellet of cocaine burst inside her. Olga Heaven says she has personally come across a number of cases where cocaine couriers have died. She recalls the case of a teenage girl from Ghana, who travelled to the UK in 2007 with several cocaine pellets concealed in her body. Ms Heaven says: 'She had swallowed the drugs in Ghana and travelled to the UK where she passed out the majority of the packages. She went back to Ghana and was with her friend on a night out. When she had an alcoholic drink, a pellet left inside her burst and she died.' The pellet had been in her body for up to two weeks before she died.

Brian Smyth says the swallowing method of smuggling is a *modus operandi* frequently used by the organisers of such trafficking attempts, who do not appear to have any compassion for the mules carrying out their orders. Many travel several thousand kilometres to deliver the drugs to the destination country, with some journeys as long as eighteen hours from areas of the Caribbean. Anxiety about the possibility of cocaine pellets exploding within their bodies results in mules being over-zealous in their rush to get through customs checks, prompting officers to become suspicious of them.

The sequence of events which can lead to a person becoming a drugs courier was the main focus of the *Maame Goes to London* campaign. The main character in the production was a Ghanaian mother of five children, who was imprisoned in Britain after she was caught smuggling cannabis into the UK from her home country. The film showed how Maame became involved in the industry after she was plunged into poverty following the death of her husband. Looking for a way out, she agreed to smuggle drugs into the UK, but she was apprehended and sentenced to a long jail term that separated her from her young children.

Customs officers' suspicions are often compounded by passenger profiling of individuals to establish their route and any unusual flight activity, such as a number of stops en route from the place of departure to the destination. Customs officers will ask people under suspicion to give a urine sample, to determine if there are drugs in their system. In Dublin Airport a special area with toilet facilities has been set aside where mules pass the drugs they have hidden internally. In some cases, however, they have to be taken to hospital for an X-ray to determine if drugs are hidden in their system, as in the case of forty-six-year-old Surinam native, Marlene Smith, and her twenty-six-year-old daughter, Mona Lisa Loe Afoe.

The Netherlands-based women were stopped coming through Dublin Airport from Dusseldorf on 27 August 2006. Searches of the women proved negative and they were taken to Beaumont Hospital for X-rays. The tests revealed that both had ingested cocaine in a bid to traffic it into Ireland. Smith had 107 pellets of the drug hidden in her stomach and intestines, worth more than €72,000. The courier was living in poverty in the Netherlands and told Gardaí that she had agreed to take part in the drugs run to raise money to return to Surinam to find her brother. Afoe had hidden fifty-five pellets in her body to help her raise money to pay off a €500 debt she owed a criminal. She had approached the drugs lord for a loan to cover her rent and utility bills. Sergeant Martin Halpin of Santry Gardaí told Dublin Circuit Criminal Court that the women were to be met on arrival in Dublin by someone who would collect the drugs from them. They both pleaded guilty to possession of cocaine for sale or supply. There was no mandatory sentence facing them for that charge, and Judge Katherine Delahunt told the court that a four-year sentence for each was justified. She said the women were selected to act as couriers because they were vulnerable.

While hiding drugs internally is viewed as a less detectable method of smuggling by drug traffickers, couriers still opt to conceal drugs in their luggage or on their person. Brian Smyth explains that there are various attempts made by smugglers to conceal the drugs. He says officers have come across cocaine diluted in liquid in bottles of drink, in packaging, toys, boxes, and in picture frames. Among the more unusual finds were in wooden legs, in wheelchairs and in babies' nappies.

In some cases, couriers are caught with drugs hidden internally as well as carrying drugs either in their luggage or on their person. Typically, this happens when a courier cannot swallow all the consignment he or she is expected to transport. In September 2006 customs officers stopped two men coming through Cork Airport on a flight from Amsterdam. A search of one of the men resulted in the discovery of a quarter of a kilo of cocaine pellets that had been strapped around his body. He and his fellow traveller were taken to Cork University Hospital after it was established they had swallowed 110 pellets of the drug between them.

Mr Smyth says it is an ever-challenging prospect for customs officers at the frontiers to be aware of the potential of literally everything being used to conceal drugs. He says drugs can be brought into a country in relatively small quantities. The purity of cocaine at smuggling point can be as high as 80 per cent, which is later broken down to as low as 20 per cent with the use of a mixing agent. Therefore, the quantity can cost up to four times more on the streets than its value before it was mixed with an agent.

One of the most intricate methods used by cocaine traffickers is converting it into liquid form and pouring it onto clothing, which is then brought into the destination country in the passenger's luggage. When the drug reaches its destination, it is reclaimed from the clothing in a complex procedure involving the use of a chemical solution, which separates the drug from the fabric. In July 2003 a Bolivian man was arrested in Kilkenny, a few days after he arrived in Ireland. Juan Carlos Melgar Alba was questioned in connection with the discovery of a large quantity of cocaine in a house in the city. Gardaí and customs officers believe the house was being used as a laboratory to remove cocaine from clothes that had been impregnated with the drug. He was handed down an eight-year prison sentence and was due for release in July 2009. However, he absconded from a prison work team in Dublin in May 2007, during temporary release granted to him from Mountjoy prison to take part in a programme in Ballymun. Despite efforts to locate him, he managed to evade the Irish authorities and is believed to have fled back to South America.

Attempts are regularly made to smuggle drugs through ferry ports, with illicit substances often hidden in cargo or concealed in panels attached to vehicles. A Polish man was sentenced to six years in prison in February 2006 after 14 million worth of cocaine was smuggled into Ireland from the Netherlands by ferry in May 2005. Marius Baran from Pila in Poland had bought a car in Germany and registered it in his wife's name in his home country. He then drove it to the Netherlands, where it was loaded with cocaine. He caught a ferry to Newcastle, in England, before driving to Stranraer, in Scotland, to catch a ferry to Belfast. He drove to Cork where he parked t,he car in a multi-storey car park in the city centre. Gardaí acting on information about the vehicle had it under surveillance in the car park when Baran, his wife and one of his children sat into it the following day. Baran was arrested and searched, but no drugs were found on his person. A sniffer dog was used to search the car and the cocaine was found in a panel built into the chassis.

Postal services are also used for the worldwide distribution of illegal substances. In October 2006 a search of a consignment of eight jackets sent from Argentina to Ireland resulted in the seizure of half a kilo of cocaine. The drug had been hidden in the buttons of the jackets and was discovered by customs officers during a search in Portlaoise.

Cocaine had become popular in Ireland in that decade, helped by the growth of the Irish economy in the late 1990s and the first years of the new millennium. The boom period provided people with extra disposable income. Until then, drug use was seen as being limited to working class areas, but the increased wealth resulted in a shift in the Irish drug culture. Cocaine became the accepted drug of the Irish middle classes, taking away the focus from the heroin-ravaged drug culture of socially-disadvantaged areas of Dublin. However, a bumper crop of opium in Afghanistan in recent years has resulted in an increased availability of heroin, resulting in use of the drug moving beyond disadvantaged areas of Dublin city. A rise in the number of middle class users smoking the drug has been seen in recent years, with seizures of the drug now being made outside the capital in areas including Tipperary, West Cork and Galway. Afghanistan is the main producer of the highly addictive drug. The UN Office on Drugs and Crime drugs report for 2007 identified that country as producing 92 per cent of the world's heroin in 2006. According to the report, opium production in Afghanistan rose by almost 50 per cent in 2006.

Drug traffickers have identified the niche in the market created by the increasing popularity of heroin in Ireland and other parts of Western Europe. The substance is being transported to the west over land, via three main routes – the Northern Balkan Route through Turkey, Bulgaria, Romania, Hungary and Austria; the Silk Road Route through central Asia into Russia, Ukraine, and central and Eastern Europe, and the Southern Balkan Route through Greece, Albania and Macedonia. According to the World Customs Report of 2006, road vehicles are mainly used for the trafficking of the drug, accounting for 73 per cent of the seizures recorded globally by customs agencies. However, the report noted an increase in couriers using air traffic from 11 per cent in 2005 to 14 per cent the following year.

The growth in production is making it easy for drug users to turn their focus to heroin. It is cheaper than cocaine, but can prove more expensive for a user because of its highly addictive nature. The difference in the new millennium is that the popularity of the drug has spread beyond Dublin into the provincial cities and towns throughout Ireland. First time users outside of the capital are not making a connection between it and the societal problems experienced in Dublin in the 1980s, when heroin use fuelled a rise in crime by addicts who needed to fund their habit. The increased availability of the drug in Ireland resulted in law enforcement agencies making regular seizures throughout the country in 2006, 2007 and 2008. In May 2008 two separate seizures of the drug were made in Dublin in two days, worth a total of €2.2 million.

Although the majority of the seizures were small, two major

consignments of the lethal drug were uncovered by customs officers at points of entry to Ireland within a couple of months of each other in 2007. The first was in June when a van was searched after coming off a ferry in Rosslare from France – 10.6kg of heroin, worth €2.1 million, was seized in that operation. Two months later, 12kg was recovered in Dublin Port, when sniffer dog Lulu carried out a routine search of two wood-burning range cookers, which had arrived from Rotterdam. When she detected the presence of drugs, customs officers found the 12kg of heroin, along with 2.5kg of cocaine. The value of the overall seizure was put at €2.6 million.

In early 2008 another massive consignment of the drug was also seized in Dublin Port in a joint operation between customs and Gardaí from the National Drugs Unit and Tallaght: 10kg of heroin, worth €2 million, was seized after a lengthy surveillance operation. The heroin was found in a false bottom of a wooden crate containing machine parts. The truck containing the crate had originated in Belgium and arrived by ferry into Dublin Port.

Preliminary results released by the Irish Revenue Commissioners in January 2008 revealed that customs officers were involved in sixty-one seizures of cocaine and heroin, worth €115 million, in 2007. The seizure of 1,550kg of cocaine off Dunlough Bay in West Cork in July 2007 helped to drive up the value of the total hauls to more than six times the value of cannabis seized in that year. Customs officers made 1,846 seizures of cannabis, showing the continued popularity of the drug, although the media concentration was focused on cocaine and heroin use.

Included in the significant cannabis hauls in that period was the discovery of €13 million worth of herbal cannabis in a 6m container, which had arrived in Dublin Port from South Africa in August. The haul weighed more than 1 tonne and was hidden in six lecture stands. The drug was found with the aid of an X-ray scanner – which confirmed suspicions about the stands. Neatly packed parcels of cannabis were discovered by customs officers when they prised open the stands.

Among the more unusual drugs being intercepted by customs officers at airports in Ireland is Khat. The plant is prohibited in Ireland since 1990, and is also illegal in the US, Canada, Norway and Sweden. Khat in its natural plant state is legal in Britain, although extract of the leaf is banned. It is very popular among African immigrants in the UK, particularly among the Somalian community. The leaf is chewed, a habit usually associated with males. Chewing releases the stimulating drug cathonine into the system. It provides a high similar to amphetamines; health concerns have resulted in its ban in several countries. Seizures of the drug in Ireland are rare, although there has been an increase in recent years. In 2001 four seizures of the drug were made by customs and had a combined value of €444,408. This was compared with eleven seizures, worth €905,000, in 2006. One of the seizures in 2006 was of approximately €12,000 worth of the drug in the luggage of two women boarding a flight from Dublin to the US in August. Sarah Rodriguez and Emma Peacock from Newcastle in England were both given three-year sentences for possession of the controlled drug before Dublin Circuit Criminal Court in March 2007. Both women had expected to get €1,000 each for importing the drug to the US.

Two months earlier €15,000 of the drug was discovered in the luggage of a British couple travelling through Dublin Airport en route from London to New York. John Maltby from Leamington Spa was sentenced to four years in prison, with two years suspended. His partner, Dawn Willoughby received a two-year suspended sentence.

Drug smuggling gangs in Africa, South America and the Caribbean are constantly recruiting people to act as mules for them. Poverty and drug addiction lead vulnerable people, such as Tonnette Andu, to respond to the offers of large sums of money. Not all couriers are caught at points of entry into Ireland and other countries, making such offers extremely tempting as a means of making easy money quickly. Even when mules are caught, they can be tempted back into the trade again because of the money and because they may not be able to get other work. However, not only do mules put their own lives at risk by smuggling drugs, like cocaine, internally but they also play a pivotal role in the supply of drugs to people whose lives are wrecked by addiction.

Chapter 2

GEMEOS

When John O'Toole went for a drink in a yacht club in Panama city in June 1997, his mind was a million miles away from his native Ireland. His beloved Panamanian wife, Gabriella, was seriously ill, battling a war against cancer. He was only beginning to adjust to life in South America after the couple had to leave the Canary Islands when faced with financial ruin after his yacht charter business failed. O'Toole was not used to failure – the Dubliner had built up the yachting company from nothing to a successful business before it eventually collapsed. Before he set up the yachting business, he had a successful decorating company employing more than fifty people.

As his friends in Ireland began to enjoy the boom times of the Celtic Tiger, John O'Toole was going through financial chaos. He would have been able to bear the pain and stress of his financial burden, if another central part of his life had not begun to crumble. When Gabriella became ill, his life fell apart. With her illness and no income in Tenerife, the O'Tooles decided to move to Gabriella's native Panama, and hope for a better life there. Becoming used to the different lifestyle was going to be difficult for the Irish man, but his draw to the sea and his background in yachting made it easier to settle in a city where he could build his social life around the yacht clubs.

It was in the bar of one of those yacht clubs in June 1997 that the fifty-year-old met a charismatic man, someone who would change his life forever. As the two men got talking, O'Toole felt he had met someone with whom he could relate, someone who would lend a listening ear for his many problems. He poured his heart out about his fears for Gabriella and the financial problems they were experiencing. He also talked about the death of his brother, Richard, who had been killed in a yachting accident in the Canaries in the mid-1990s. In the course of the conversation the enigmatic man made it clear to O'Toole that he was a player in the international drugs scene, which O'Toole later claimed shocked him. However, he still fell for the charms of the trafficker. Incredibly, he seemed to believe there would be no negative impact on his life by his association with him, despite being asked to become a player in his empire. The trafficker, later to become known as Mr X, offered O'Toole a role in his business as a way out of his financial abyss. He asked O'Toole to help take a quantity of drugs to Europe from South America. O'Toole later said he was shocked by the request and that he had never been approached like that before. He said he refused point blank to become involved.

The refusal did not seem to damage the budding friendship. Although their relationship was barely a couple of hours old, the Dubliner could see that his plight had tugged at the heartstrings of his new associate, who told him he did not want to see him stuck. As the night drew to a close in the club, the rich man took O'Toole to his hotel room where he gave him $5,000 to help pay for the cancer treatment of a woman he had never met, with no apparent strings attached. If his recollection of events are to believed, the Irish man appeared at this point to be either too naïve or blinded by his financial troubles to realise that accepting the money was the first step towards becoming involved in Mr X's drug trafficking operation. O'Toole later claimed he thought his new friend was joking when he offered him the money and he also said he did not know there would be conditions attached to the payment. Despite the man being a relative stranger, he accepted the payment in a desperate bid to turn the lives of his family around. He later made it appear he had fooled himself into believing the money had really been given without strings attached and that he would not be asked again to become involved in Mr X's operations. Looking back on that first meeting, he later said that he thought his new acquaintance was genuinely sorry for the O'Tooles and that he wanted to help.

That initial payment became the start of a cycle which saw O'Toole becoming more and more financially dependent on his Panama godfather. Payments totalling $70,000 were made to O'Toole over the next year for no obvious reason, with instalments of $4,000 and $5,000 being paid once a month. Even if the Dubliner did not realise it, the financial good times could not continue to roll for him, if his benefactor was not to get something back from an arrangement which had so far been a one-way street. Despite the regular payments, from the drug lord, the O'Tooles still had not found a way out of their financial mess and Gabriella's treatment was continuing. A year on from their first meeting, he now felt confident enough to ask his South American friend for more money, instead of waiting to be offered a payment by the magnate. He knew the money was the proceeds of drug dealing, yet appeared not to consider other options, such as selling a Spanish-registered catamaran they owned, called the *Gemeos*. O'Toole had brought the vessel to Panama with him when he left Tenerife.

Asking Mr X for more money was a dangerous move. By this stage, the godfather figure had O'Toole's situation sussed and he had the Irish man where he wanted him. O'Toole had already done one job for Mr X – he had travelled to Amsterdam at the start of 1998 to meet with one of Mr X's contacts to discuss the conveying of drugs in containers. O'Toole said he later saw the same contact in Panama. According to the *Examiner*, Irish authorities later alleged that O'Toole had paid a man $40,000 on one occasion, knowing it was the proceeds of drug dealing. During the trip to Europe, the Irish man spent a few days in the Netherlands before flying to Dublin and visiting Kinsale, en route back to Panama.

Having already carried out this job for his benefactor, O'Toole could not have been surprised when Mr X decided to enlist him in a drug smuggling operation. The Panamanian knew that even though the O'Tooles were strapped for cash, they had one very valuable asset – the *Gemeos*. Despite their financial difficulties, they had not sold the vessel, information which the Panamanian-based benefactor used to his advantage during that meeting in June 1998. He asked O'Toole to use the 15m *Gemeos* to take a consignment of drugs to Kinsale, in his native Ireland, in return for a pay-off of $300,000. Although O'Toole had visited Kinsale months earlier during his trip to Ireland, he claimed that visit was unrelated to the voyage he was now being enlisted in.

The drug lord said the overall payment for the latest trip would incorporate the $70,000 already paid to O'Toole during the previous twelve months. He promised that the remaining $230,000 would be paid over when the job was completed. The 'Mr Nice Guy' routine was over and the process was underway to enlist the Irish man into a major international drug smuggling operation. He was now facing three choices – sell the *Gemeos,* do the job or face death. With his wife already in the clutches of a terminal condition, he had the future of his two young children depending on his decision. But which was the right choice to make? Selling the boat did not seem to enter his mind. With that ruled out, there was no contest between the other two choices. If he didn't do what his benefactor was asking, he was facing murder. The much-needed money for Gabriella's treatment was not available from another source.

In a statement made to Gardaí in Ireland three months later and reported in the *Examiner*, O'Toole recalled of that meeting: 'This time, I asked him for cash. He said to take the boat to Europe or "I will take the boat and you are dead". This man then attacked me and beat me up in a car park in Panama City.' He also alleged that the man threatened to shoot him if he did not carry out his wishes. O'Toole added: 'I agreed to go as I felt I had no choice and needed cash to treat my wife's cancer.' He said the money would have helped his family in a big way.

O'Toole told Mr X he would take the cocaine on board the *Gemeos* into Ireland through the harbour town of Kinsale. Known today as the gourmet capital of Ireland, Kinsale is also famous for the arrival of an armada of Spanish boats in 1601 to aid the Irish chieftains battling against the English. The Spanish had hoped to use Ireland as a means of progressing towards defeating the English in the Anglo-Spanish war, which was in essence a battle between Protestant England and Catholic Spain. For Mr X, historic Kinsale was to be the landing point for a cocaine shipment destined mainly for the UK and Europe.

Having reluctantly agreed to carry out the dangerous deed,

another crew member now had to be found to assist in the illegal mission. Involved already was a Welsh man, who O'Toole had known in Tenerife and who had also moved to Panama. He had also worked in the maritime industry in Tenerife. According to O'Toole's version of events, the Welsh man had known Mr X, which is how O'Toole became acquainted with him initially. With the Welsh man and O'Toole both ready for the smuggling job, a friendship forged during the men's time in the Canaries was brought into play. Englishman Michael Tune had been a coal miner in Britain for eighteen years before losing his job. As a result, he went from job to job, with nothing steady to fall back on. He moved to Tenerife, where he first met O'Toole and the Welsh man. According to Tune, the Welsh man had earlier asked him if he had ever considered taking drugs on a boat. Tune said he would consider the suggestion and eventually became involved in the Kinsale plan as he had no job. The timing could not have been better for thirty-eight-year-old Tune. His girlfriend had given birth to their first child and he could not see how the family unit could have a stable life with no regular income. The $100,000 promised for helping in the drugs operation with which O'Toole was involved was too much to refuse, so Tune agreed to sail with the dodgy consignment on board the *Gemeos*. O'Toole's role became that of skipper, while Tune was a crewman, along with the Welsh man.

With the crew selected, the next step was to load the *Gemeos* with its precious and illegal cargo. A number of men involved in Mr X's operation loaded more than 300 grey packets of cocaine, each the size of a videotape and weighing a kilo, on to the catamaran. They paid careful attention to hiding the valuable packages. Secret compartments were used to hide them, making them invisible to the naked eye. In some areas of the boat, liquid foam was used to seal the drugs into place. When dry, the foam gave the impression of solid panels, neatly disguising the cargo. Two compartments were located under two bunk beds in the main cabin of the vessel, as well as under the floor and behind bulkheads. The loading operation took place over a number of weeks. O'Toole helped on one occasion, carrying drugs from a car onto the *Gemeos*. Eventually, the illicit work was done and it was time to hand over the reins to O'Toole and his two crewmen. No risk could be taken in the next step of the operation and he was given specific and firm directions on what to do once the *Gemeos* sailed into Kinsale harbour. A mobile phone number was given to him, of a man who was expecting the cargo in the Cork town. O'Toole was to ring the number when he arrived, to alert the man that the *Gemeos* had arrived.

The risky voyage from Panama to Ireland was not only a new experience for the men, who brought the *Gemeos* through the Caribbean, the Azores and the Canaries before arriving into Kinsale on 1 September 1998, but one which must have made them question their actions. As they sailed into the harbour, their thoughts were on each of their own situations, with hopes that within days, their roles in the tricky operation would be over and they would be rich men. How they would feel about spending tainted money was a question only they could answer. For O'Toole, the trip made the prospect of Gabriella's recovery more of a reality. But as they sailed into their destination, the *Gemeos* experienced engine trouble and the crew had to alert local man Billy O'Brien to their plight. Mr O'Brien was out on the water with his speedboat when he saw the *Gemeos's* signal, requesting him to tow the vessel into the harbour. He towed the catamaran and its crew into Kinsale, where the vessel was then tied to a mooring in the Middle Cove. Unluckily for the crew, two key aspects of the boat's arrival raised the concerns of harbourmaster, Captain Phil Devitt, that there was something unusual about the catamaran. Captain Devitt wondered why they had not alerted harbour authorities or paid harbour dues for using the mooring. He also noted that the private landing area was belonging to another boat and the *Gemeos* should not have been moored there.

More crucially, however, was the absence of a Q flag on the vessel. All vessels arriving into a new port are required to fly such a flag, also called the Quarantine flag. By flying the Q, crews of vessels are alerting local customs officials that they have come in from abroad. A decision had been taken not to fly the flag or pay the harbour dues so as not to alert customs officers about their arrival. Flying the Q flag would have been an open invitation to customs to come on board – not something which could be risked with such a large quantity of drugs on board. However, the decisions were poorly made as they ended up attracting unwarranted attention. When the crew of the *Gemeos* failed to fly the Q flag, suspicions were raised and the vessel was put under surveillance by customs and excise officials on 2 September. The flag was later found hidden in a drawer. Customs officers boarded the vessel on 3 September. With such a massive shipment, it was hardly surprising that the team in Panama had been prepared for a search of the ship and that the crew on board had taken steps to avoid a search. Those who had loaded the drugs on the *Gemeos* had not taken any chances in their attempts to conceal the drug, and efforts by the customs and excise team to find contraband on the catamaran failed dismally. The usually dependable sniffer dog Dusty was brought on board to smell his way through the boat, but his efforts also failed. By this point, the boarding party were frustrated as they knew there was something suspicious about the vessel and its crew. In covering the case, the *Examiner* reported that customs officer, Christopher Fitzpatrick, said: 'My belief was that there may have been drugs on board but that they were already gone.'

Their unease was not helped by the skipper, O'Toole. Why was he telling them the vessel's voyage had originated in Tenerife when charts on the catamaran showed it had travelled through the Caribbean, 644km east of the Bahamas, a month before arriving into Kinsale? Christopher Fitzpatrick set out to find out why, when speaking to O'Toole. He was one of the first members of the investigation teams to speak with the Dubliner. During their conversation, O'Toole told him he had planned to sell the boat in Europe and had sailed it from Tenerife to Ireland before the sale. The skipper also claimed to have taken the *Gemeos* northwest to the Azores to get better winds for the journey to Kinsale, which he said had taken him and his crew twenty days. He had laid out a detailed story of the trip, possibly in the hope that it would have been enough to convince officers to trust his version and not to check the charts on board. He said that the voyage had not gone any further west in the Atlantic than the Azores – despite marks on the charts found on board showing the route through the Caribbean. The customs officer pushed the issue and O'Toole at this point said he had taken the boat from his wife and sailed it across the Atlantic to sell in Europe. Sticking to his story that the boat was going to be sold on arrival in Europe, the Dubliner said he was hoping to get £150,000 for the catamaran.

In essence, his explanations were not convincing enough to persuade the investigating customs and excise team and Gardaí not to carry out intricate searches of the boat. The customs and excise rummage team got a search underway, by members who had been sent to a centre of excellence in the

UK for specialist training. This training had provided them with the know-how to locate hidden drugs on board sea vessels including oil tankers, pleasure craft and everything in between. In the case of the *Gemeos*, the training paid off. The first packets of a suspect white powder were found under a plywood base in the port cabin bunk area on 4 September. A further rummage revealed more packets in the starboard cabin, and under diesel tanks in a forward annex of the boat. As the rummage got underway, John O'Toole and Michael Tune started to worry that their neat little plan was falling asunder. By now, the Welsh man had left Kinsale. He had flown out of Dublin airport to the US on 3 September. He was detained briefly by authorities in Dublin airport but was allowed leave the country, as the drugs had not been found on board the *Gemeos* by then. He was never questioned about the find on the *Gemeos*.

As the Welsh man was leaving Ireland, O'Toole and Tune were coming under more and more pressure. Gardaí had decided to search their accommodation. A revolver, fifty rounds of ammunition, hand-cuffs and two cans of pepper spray were found in Tune's room in a local guesthouse, which he had booked into under an assumed name. Tune told Gardaí he had the gun because he was afraid of pirates around Cuba. He said he bought it from a Panamanian man he met with the Welsh man. He told Gardaí he had paid $400 for the gun and that the handcuffs and spray had come as part of the deal.

As they were being taken into custody in Kinsale for fire-arms offences, the 'Mr Big', who had overseen the operation, was beginning to count his losses from the safety of his base in Panama, where Gabriella O'Toole was still gravely ill. Neither man made contact with Mr X while in custody, but it is thought he had been informed almost immediately of the loss of the drugs by the person waiting to hear from the crew when they arrived in Ireland. The two men were taken to Bandon Garda station for questioning about the find, while their thoughts focused on what might have been if the operation had gone according to plan. They knew that if the cocaine was found, then neither man would get the financial rewards promised by Mr X. There was also the fear of imprisonment and separation from their families.

As they began to panic, customs officers and Gardaí con-tinued with their investigations in Kinsale. An in-depth search of the catamaran continued, while the men were in cus-tody, by officers delighted that they had persevered in their search. Once the initial discovery was made, two decisions were taken. The two arrested suspects were released from questioning on firearms offences at lunchtime that day, but were re-arrested immediately for questioning drugs offences under the Criminal Justice (Drug Trafficking) Act 1996. To facilitate the on-going search of O'Toole's vessel, a decision was taken to remove it from the Middle Cove mooring to a private boatyard in the town. The yard was sealed off to prevent members of the curious public from entering the area.

Careful work by the search teams yielded further results the next day and again on 6 September. A seizure of 140kg was taken from the vessel on the second search day, while 20kg were removed on the third. Gardaí and customs officers were themselves aware that the product they had in their possession was cocaine. However, a quantity of the drugs was sent for forensic analysis in the garda forensic laboratory, in Dublin, to confirm their view and to put a value on it. Pressure was mounting in Bandon Garda station, where the two men were being interviewed. Time was running out and it was decided to apply to the courts for an extension to the men's period of detention, to enable the Gardaí to further the case. The two men were brought before Judge Brendan Wallace at a special sitting of Bandon District Court on 6 September, where Chief Superintendent Adrian Culligan applied to have their period of detention extended by three days under the Criminal Justice (Drug Trafficking) Act. The application was granted and the in-depth questioning continued. As O'Toole began to reveal to Gardaí about his dealings with the Panamanian godfather figure, other officers concentrated on the international picture. Enquiries were made through Interpol about the backgrounds of the two, to determine if they had form in the drug trafficking scene and to establish the route taken by the *Gemeos* to Ireland. The investigation also centred on the Welsh man's whereabouts, but attempts to trace him failed.

Efforts were also concentrated on the gang behind the Kinsale seizure and officers believe Mr X was a member of a major drugs cartel based in South America. O'Toole told them that the Panamanian godfather had a contact in Kinsale who had Colombian connections. He also claimed that he may have had ancestors from Ireland. Mr X was never questioned by Gardaí about the haul – sources said there was not enough evidence to extradite him to Ireland in connection with the *Gemeos* venture.

As the end of the three extra days of detention came near, investigating Gardaí and customs officials felt they had enough evidence to charge them both. Two charges each were brought against the men by the Director of Public Prosecutions (DPP) on behalf of the Irish State, and two further charges were brought by customs and excise. The DPP's charges under the Misuse of Drugs Act were the importation of cocaine between 1 and 4 September, and possession of the drug for sale or supply at Kinsale harbour, between the same dates. The customs and excise charges were brought under the Customs Consolidation Act, in relation to being knowingly concerned with the importation of cocaine into the Irish State and being knowingly concerned in dealing with controlled drugs on 2 September. O'Toole and Tune were both horrified by the decision to charge them. Their hopes of coming into Kinsale unnoticed had been dashed and now they were facing imprisonment in Ireland while awaiting trial. When the customs and excise charges were put to him in Bandon Garda station, O'Toole replied: 'Not guilty'. Tune said, 'No.'

Both were strangers to west Cork but were rapidly getting to know landmarks, such as the Garda station and courthouse in Bandon. For the second time in three days, they were brought before the court in the town, again before Judge Brendan Wallace. The difference this time round was that the men's identities could now be revealed to a public fascinated by the recovery of the cocaine from the *Gemeos* in Kinsale that week. Photographers waited outside the court to get the first shots of the two men, who tried to keep their faces covered when entering and leaving the court. Both men's addresses highlighted the global significance of the Kinsale haul. O'Toole's address was in Panama city, although he also had an address in Enniskerry, County Wicklow. Tune's supplied address was in Los Americas, Tenerife.

During the short hearing, Detective Sergeant Sean Healy and Garda Donal McCarthy gave evidence of arresting, charging and cautioning the two men on behalf of the DPP. Judge Wallace referred to the varying reports of the haul made in the media, and asked what was the exact value of the seizure. State solicitor for West Cork, Malachy Boohig, said the estimated value at that point was £100 million. Applications were made for free legal aid by solicitors for both men. No objection was put up against the request. Although both men had addresses that were indicative of a high life in sunny climes, the court heard that they had no visible assets. Mr Boohig said enquiries revealed that the only asset which O'Toole had was the *Gemeos*. But ownership of the boat was now of little use to the fifty-one-year-old skipper – the boat had been seized by customs and excise during the drug recovery operation and could not be considered an asset by O'Toole. The State solicitor's word on the men's lack of financial means was accepted, but Judge Wallace warned that free legal aid would be revoked if further enquiries revealed that the men had assets.

An application by the men's solicitors to grant the men bail was contested by the State, and Judge Wallace remanded both men in custody to appear at a sitting of Clonakilty District Court six days later. From then on, the world of prison, courthouses and remand hearings became the norm for the two men as they waited on a date for the trial, which they hoped would give them freedom. Each day spent in prison was spent thinking of how they would by now have been re-united with their families – if the shipment had not been seized by the Irish authorities, or if they had not undertaken the mission in the first place. For John O'Toole, each day in his native Ireland was a day apart from the Panamanian wife whose life he had hoped to save with money earned through the *Gemeos* operation. And as Tune served his remand, waiting for their trial to kick off, he was missing the first landmarks of his baby's life. His decision to make money quickly through involvement in the drugs run had backfired.

The days turned into months and the two men spent Christmas alone in prison in Ireland, as their families tried to get on with their lives in Tenerife and Panama. Gabriella was still struggling in her fight against cancer but tried to keep in contact with her husband through letters.

A new year dawned and the prosecution case against the men had been built. The case was then sent forward to the Circuit Criminal Court sessions taking place in May in Cork city. With investigations having extended from Ireland to the Canaries, the Caribbean and South America, and the men not having pleaded guilty, it was expected that the trial could last for several weeks. The opening of the trial on 4 May was the start of a media frenzy – which was to last throughout the trial. A fifth charge was also being faced by the men – that of having more than £10,000 worth of cocaine for sale or supply. This charge had a mandatory sentence of ten years, unless there were any special circumstances. Local reporters, who regularly attended hearings in the Cork court, were joined by their colleagues from national daily newspapers and broadcast outlets. Reporters, photographers and television crews kept sentry at the court throughout the trial, waiting to get the next gem of information to satisfy their waiting readers and listeners. Nine men and three women were selected to the jury for what was one of the most high-profile cases ever seen in Cork. Jury members were warned that the case would take at least three weeks, with the possibility of it lasting a lot longer.

As the media, prosecution, defence team and Michael Tune got psyched up for the opening day of the trial John O'Toole had been dealt a shattering blow. Gabriella's fight against cancer was failing as the trial approached and he received a last heartbreaking letter from her in the run up to the opening day. Four days before the trial opened on 4 May, Gabriella passed away as her husband's legal team prepared his defence. Ironically, although her life was over, her presence hung over the trial as O'Toole's defence team appealed for the jury's sense of empathy for their client.

Senior counsel John Edwards was the first to speak in the trial. Opening the case to the court, he said: 'On or about 1 September 1998, a sailing vessel known as the *Gemeos*, sailed into Kinsale Harbour. It was a catamaran, a twin hulled boat bridged by a structure holding the two together. It has a mast and sails. When a sailing vessel comes in from abroad, it must present itself for a customs inspection. The manner in which this is done is that it runs up a flag known as a Q flag, which indicates to the customs authority that it has come in from abroad. The *Gemeos* did not fly a Q flag. It came to the attention of the local customs officers and suspicions were aroused.' With those words, quoted in the *Examiner's* coverage of the trial, the way was paved for the unfolding of an international story that had put Kinsale in the spotlight as a drop off point by a gang operating a global cocaine smuggling industry.

In his opening speech, he alleged that Tune and O'Toole

and another man, not before the court, were the crew of the *Gemeos*. He related how a large quantity of cocaine – 320kg in all – was found contained in small packages concealed on board the catamaran. He said it had taken the searchers a lot of time to uncover the hidden stash. The haul had then been sent to the national forensic science laboratory in Dublin, where the cocaine was found to be 75 per cent pure. The purity had enabled the prosecution to estimate the value of the haul at £41 million, a considerable reduction from the £100 million estimate supplied by State solicitor Malachy Boohig to the initial court hearing in the case, when the two men appeared at Bandon District Court the previous September.

Customs and excise officers had played a huge role in the recovery operation and a lot of attention was focused on them in the trial. Christopher Fitzpatrick detailed his interaction with O'Toole shortly after the arrival of the *Gemeos* in Kinsale. He and his colleague, Patrick O'Sullivan, admitted that there was no obvious appearance of drugs on the boat when they carried out preliminary examinations. Another customs witness, Edward Hogan, agreed with defence barrister Tom Creed that the drugs would not have been visible to the crew while sailing and working the boat.

Also giving evidence for the prosecution was Marie Comer from Southampton. She told the court that her records from the Belmont Yacht Master Academy in Southampton showed that Tune had a certificate from the academy, after doing an introduction to sailing training course in May 1998. The £500 course was done four months before the arrival of the *Gemeos* into Kinsale. Tune had given the academy an address in Ash Crescent, Mexborough, South Yorkshire.

Her evidence came at a turning point in the trial. Later that day, Judge Patrick J. Moran told the jury that legal argument would have to take place in their absence and told them their presence in court would not be required for a week. It was at this point that, unknown to the jury, Tune's part in the trial came to an end. In their absence, he pleaded guilty to the charges of importing cocaine and being in possession of the drug with intent to supply at Kinsale, County Cork. He was no longer in the courtroom while the trial of O'Toole progressed. The jury was not told of Tune's guilty plea. The members were told that they should not speculate on the reason why he was no longer on trial. Telling them that he had pleaded guilty may have worked to cloud their judgement while deliberating on O'Toole's case. An order was also made by Judge Moran banning the media from publishing Tune's plea, on the basis that it could influence their deliberations. The focus of the trial was now solely on the skipper – who did not echo Tune's guilty plea.

The trial got underway again with the statement made by O'Toole to investigating Gardaí in which he detailed getting involved in the *Gemeos* mission after meeting Mr X in the yacht club bar in Panama city, almost two years before the trial. According to the *Examiner,* he told Gardaí: 'This man asked me would I take some stuff to Europe. I knew it was drugs he was referring to and I said no. I spent a good few hours with him and he knew I had cash difficulties with my business and my wife's cancer condition also, as I mentioned those things to him.' The statement detailed how Mr X then gave him the first payment of $5,000, building up to an overall payments of $70,000, before the voyage to Kinsale was arranged in June 1998. O'Toole also told officers that he had no previous convictions and that the voyage to Kinsale was a once off.

After his statement was read out, O'Toole took the stand and said he was shocked by the initial approach made to him by Mr X about transporting drugs. He said: 'I was sort of shocked – I had never been approached like that before. I refused point blank.' He added in answer to cross-examination by Mr Edwards: 'I made it plain that I did not want to get involved – I never thought it would come to what it did – it was a nightmare. I thought at the time that he was genuinely sorry for me and my wife, and he had money and he wanted to help.' Despite his involvement in the drug trafficking operation, he told the court that he did not approve of drug dealing. He said: 'I don't like drug dealers because of what they do – it's all Mafiosi, gangs, killings and that sort of thing. I don't agree with it – it's just not in me – drugs are totally wrong and are bad for people and dangerous.'

Above: Cocaine found in a button of a jacket by customs. (Courtesy of Revenue Commissioners.)

Below: Cocaine being taken from Tonette Andu's hairstyle. (Courtesy of Revenue Commissioners.)

Above: Cocaine found on board the *Gemeos*. (Courtesy of Paddy O'Sullivan.)

Below: The interior of the *Gemeos*. (Courtesy of Paddy O'Sullivan.)

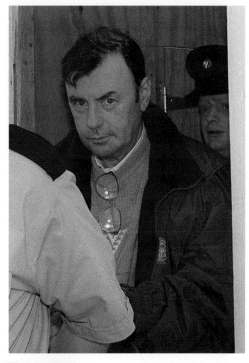

Right: John O'Toole, skipper of the *Gemeos*. (Courtesy of the *Evening Echo/Irish Examiner*.)

Left: Michael Tune, convicted for involvement in the *Gemeos* operation. (Courtesy of the *Evening Echo/Irish Examiner*.)

Left: A search is undertaken on board the *Tia*. (Courtesy of the *Evening Echo/Irish Examiner*.)

Below: John Ewart, also known as Gordon Richards, the skipper of the *Sea Mist*. (Courtesy of the *Evening Echo/Irish Examiner*.)

Above: The *Sea Mist*, in which 599kg of cocaine was found in 1996. (Courtesy of Paddy O'Sullivan.)

Below: A model of the *Sea Mist*, made by its skipper, John Ewart, while in prison. (Courtesy of Paddy O'Sullivan.)

Above: Cocaine hidden in a shaft, which had had been concealed by the spice rack in the *Sea Mist*. (Courtesy of Paddy O'Sullivan.)

Below: Sergeant Eugene O'Sullivan with the *Brime*, on which cannabis was found. (Courtesy of Eugene O'Sullivan.)

Above: Richard Preece, sitting on bales of drugs on board the *Posidonia*. (Courtesy of Provision.)

Below: The *Brime* sailing to Haulbowline naval base from Fenit. (Courtesy of Eugene O'Sullivan.)

Above: A Garda on board the *Gerry's 1*, the smaller vessel searched before the arrival of the *Brime* off the Kerry coast. (Courtesy of Eugene O'Sullivan.)

Below: Customs officers on board the *Karma of the East*. (Courtesy of Paddy O'Sullivan.)

Although O'Toole confesssed in his statements to Gardaí being involved in the operation, his defence centred on the pressures brought to bear on him by Mr X. He and his team hoped that despite his confession, the jury would look at the skipper and see a man recently bereaved, who had only become involved in the drugs mission in a bid to save his wife's life.

The prosecution were aiming to take the jury away from a sympathetic approach to the case. They hoped the jury would not look at the skipper and see a naïve and bereaved man, who was hoping he could get away with his involvement in the cocaine shipment. In his closing statement for the prosecution, Mr Edwards said the key issue for the jury to consider was whether the *Gemeos*'s skipper had been put under duress to take part in the international drug smuggling attempt. Describing O'Toole's efforts to defend his actions, Mr Edwards said: 'The accused presented a pathetic figure who dug a great big hole for himself and lost everything.' He said the jury did not have to concern themselves with whether O'Toole brought the *Gemeos* to Ireland, whether it was packed with cocaine and whether he knew it was on board, because the accused had already admitted those things. He said: 'The issue is this: is Mr O'Toole, by virtue of the fact that he contends that he was forced to be involved in this, entitled to be acquitted on the grounds of duress.' This led him to focus on the character known only as Mr X. Referring to him, Mr

Edwards said: 'The very first time he met Mr X, Mr X told him of his involvement in drug dealing. Why did he not make his excuses and leave? He got $5,000 in a hotel room in the knowledge that he (Mr X) was a drug dealer.' He went on to reveal to the jury about the $40,000 payment O'Toole had made to another man before becoming involved in the gemeos operation, knowing it was the proceeds of drug dealing. Mr Edwards also said the jury had to consider if the accused failed to take opportunities to escape from duress by contacting the authorities either in South America or in Ireland.

Mr Edwards said that the law protected against every accused man admitting guilt. He said what weighed against the duress defence was whether the accused had voluntarily become involved in a criminal gang or organisation, 'where a person puts himself in a situation where he is likely to be subjected to duress'. He said the accused had become involved with people he regarded as Mafiosa, people who were dangerous, ruthless and greedy. He sympathised with O'Toole on the death of Gabriella but he said the jury must not approach the case with sympathy. He also warned that the twelve jurors should not consider any strong personal feelings about the dangers of drug dealing.

Senior defence counsel Blaise O'Carroll was the last to address the court. In his closing statement, he appealed to the jury on behalf of O'Toole to consider the role played by Mr X.

He asked the jury to consider what kind of character the anonymous Panamanian godfather was. He said he appeared to be a generous benefactor, who was as 'sweet as pie' and appeared to be concerned about the Dubliner's wife. Mr O'Carroll continued: 'He has his own hidden agenda. He is like a cat playing with a mouse in a playful and gentle way. But when the time comes he has no difficulty reaching out his claw in a striking gesture to grab his prey. Mr O'Toole found himself like an addict owing money to this person, to be told if you do not do it I will steal your boat, I will kill you, I will kill your wife and I will kill your children. It is a classic case of where the defence of duress is appropriate.'

As O'Toole sat in the courtroom, he knew that time was ticking for him. The jury members were being addressed by Judge Moran, ahead of being sent out to consider a verdict. He hoped and prayed that the jury would look favourably on him by returning a not-guilty verdict. He listened as Judge Moran said only two of the original charges brought before him were to be considered in the case. As a result, the jury had to consider O'Toole's guilt on the charge of importing cocaine and being in possession of it with intent to supply at Kinsale the previous September. Judge Moran said the accused had been caught red-handed and the issue for the jury was whether he had been put under duress.

For four hours, he waited tensely as the jurors deliberated on the evidence before them. When the jury returned to the courtroom without a verdict that evening, they were sent to a hotel for the night. Although the following day was a Saturday, when courts in Ireland do not usually sit, the main parties in the trial returned to the Circuit Criminal Court to await the jury's decision. In just under an hour, the jurors had completed almost five hours of deliberations on the evidence and had reached a verdict. As they returned to the courtroom, O'Toole waited with bated breath. But the result was not what he had hoped for – the jury's foreman told the court that O'Toole had been found guilty of the two charges. It was only at that point that Judge Moran allowed the jurors to hear that Tune had pleaded guilty to the same two charges, half way through the trial.

Both men were due to be sentenced at a hearing of the circuit court over a week later, on 1 June 1999. The international elements of the case were once again to the fore for the sentencing hearing when the Dubliner's defence team revealed it had not been possible to get character witnesses from Scotland, Tenerife and Panama to attend. His senior counsel, Blaise O'Carroll, applied to the court for an adjournment in the case of his client, which was granted by Judge Moran. But the judge was critical of the application. Quoted in the *Examiner*, he said: 'We have had a full trial. Every aspect of the defence that could possibly be raised was raised. It was open to you to carry out all sorts of enquiries over the past ten days. We have been virtually around the world in this case. Evidence suddenly arrived very quickly from strange places. Why that information cannot be obtained now is beyond me.' Although Tune's senior counsel, Ciaran O'Loughlin, said his client was ready, Judge Moran said he would sentence both men on 11 June, as he did not want to treat the case on a piecemeal basis. Sentencing would go ahead whether or not the character witnesses were available for O'Toole.

One character witness got into the stand, on behalf of the Dubliner, when the next sentencing hearing got underway. He was Thomas Roche, a man who had become friendly with O'Toole in Tenerife. He said he could not believe that such a normal family man, like his friend, could get himself into such a situation. Once again, the issue of duress was raised when he said: 'I have to believe he was coerced in some way into this stupidity.'

Although O'Toole had spoken in court during his trial, he did not take the stand during the sentencing hearing. Tune did, however. In his statement to the court, he spoke of his regret at having becoming involved in the *Gemeos* operation. He said: 'Through stupidity I got involved in all this which I deeply regret now. There is one thing I can say to everyone, I have never been in trouble before and I never will be again.' He had been in custody in Ireland since 4 September the previous year, and he told the court that he was finding it difficult because his girlfriend and eighteen-month-old baby daughter remained in Tenerife. He said his girlfriend could only afford to make one visit to him and that members of his own family had not contacted him. In a bid to have as lenient a sentence as possible imposed on Tune, his senior counsel reminded the judge of Tune's guilty plea. He also highlighted other factors which should be considered by Judge Moran, namely his lack of previous convictions and the likelihood of him never offending again. Mirroring the drama of the *Gemeos* operation, O'Toole's counsel included Shakespeare in his plea for his client, by quoting a section of Portia's speech on the quality of mercy in 'The Merchant of Venice'.

But Judge Moran was not swayed. He referred to the illegal drugs industry as evil. He said: 'This evil causes misery, ruin, upset and carnage on decent people and their families and they bring enormous financial gain to drug barons, and in this case their carriers.' He added: 'I must send a message to people in the drugs world on behalf of people in society.' He said that the tragedies which had befallen O'Toole – including the deaths of his wife and his brother, Richard – were very moving. He said that one would have to be 'very cold' not to be moved by a letter written to the skipper by the late Gabriella. But he said it was his duty to put emotion to one side and instead focus on the very serious nature of the criminal act carried out by Tune and O'Toole. He sentenced the former English coal miner to fourteen years in prison, and gave the skipper a twenty-year sentence. He made an order requiring the State to destroy the seizure of cocaine and also sanctioned the sale of the *Gemeos* yacht by the Revenue Commissioners.

For O'Toole, the outcome was devastating. Unlike Tune, he had not admitted guilty to the two charges he was convicted of, even though he had outlined in statements to Gardaí how he had become involved in the operation. He launched an appeal against the conviction. The factors put forward for the appeal included his imprisonment in Ireland during his wife's funeral, making it impossible for him to attend. His co-operation with investigating Gardaí, his lack of previous convictions and his imprisonment since September 1998 were also included as key factors by his defence team. When the case came before the Court of Criminal Appeal, leave to appeal the conviction was refused. But four years were taken off the original sentence of twenty years, with the remaining sixteen years backdated to September 1998. The now sixty-year-old widower is serving his sentence in Portlaoise prison, thousands of kilometres away from the yacht club where he first met Mr X. He is due for release in September 2010. His children remained in Panama where they were being cared for by his wife's family following her death.

For his part, Tune was devastated at the length of his sentence, despite his guilty plea. He also lodged an appeal, but only against the severity of the sentence. The Court of Criminal Appeal ruled on 24 May 2001 that he should instead serve twelve years in prison, also backdated to September 1998. He applied to be repatriated to the UK and his application was granted in 2003. He was due for release in late 2007.

Chapter 3

SEA MIST

Gordon Richards stared at the phone in shock, wondering what to do next. His first mate had just given him the worst news he could receive. Minutes before, his priority had been to enjoy the few days he would be in Cork city while receiving treatment for backache. Now, his concern was to get new accommodation for himself, his girlfriend and her child in a bid to hide from the Irish authorities. Cork's motto of providing a safe harbour for all ships had failed for the crew of the Norwegian-registered *Sea Mist*.

Richards and his four crewmates had arrived into Cork harbour two days before, on Friday, 27 September 1996. Pulling into the harbour seemed the logical thing to do when the *Sea Mist*'s engine began to give trouble close to the Cork coast. The vessel had come a long way from Venezuela, en route to co-ordinates at sea, near the French town of Brest, and the engine problem was not the only difficulty they had to consider. The fifty-two-year-old Richards needed physiotherapy for his aching back. This, coupled with the crew's longing for fresh food, had also made it seem that Ireland was the answer to all their problems.

However, while Richards was safely ensconced in a room in Jurys Hotel on Cork's Western Road, three of his crew were being questioned by customs officers and Gardaí, who were curious about the arrival of the converted trawler into the pier between Aghada and East Ferry. The crew had earlier dropped the skipper ashore on a nearby marina. The arrival of the 18m vessel into the harbour had aroused the suspicions of at least one local man. He had knowledge of the ground where the vessel was at anchor. He recognised that the vessel was in an area of rough ground where fishermen dropped their pots. The coastal source could also see that the vessel was a type of houseboat, which was unusual to the area. He decided to disclose the information to the authorities in charge of drugs interdiction and logged a call with customs in Cork early the following morning. A customs crew was tasked to travel to the harbour area and place surveillance on the ship as it lay docked at the marina in Aghada.

The customs had spotted that the ship was flying neither the Irish flag nor the Q flag. By opting not to fly the flag, it was hoped that the vessel could creep into Cork harbour without attracting unwanted attention from customs. Because the boat was clearly newly-arrived, the absence of the flags triggered a feeling that all was not as it should be on board the boat.

On the *Sea Mist*, the three remaining crew members went about their duties blissfully unaware that their arrival had sparked concerns on land. They were keeping in regular contact with Richards by phone as he and his nineteen-year-old girlfriend, Theresa da Silva Roy, relaxed in Cork city with her two-year-old son. They had spent a difficult few days on the way into Cork and were thankful for the break from rough seas. The men decided to go ashore at East Ferry marina, with the aid of a small rib on board. When they arrived at the marina they were informed that customs wanted to speak to them at Aghada pier. They returned to their vessel for their passports and then met customs at Aghada. Two experienced customs officers met one of the crew on the pier and posed several questions about the *Sea Mist*'s voyage and her crew. When asked about their reasons for being in Cork, the men said they were en route to a shipyard in the Kiel Canal in the North Sea. When the men could not name their destination village, the customs team mentally noted that this was one more reason to question the origins of the vessel, its true destination and the cargo it had on board.

When the customs officers met the three crew members, there was another factor which prompted alarms bells to ring. The crew was made up of mixed nationalities. The man in charge at the time of their visit was not the captain. He was the first mate. He had an address in St Lucia, as had his crewmate. The third man on board was from Cumbria. The men told heir visitors of their skipper's back troubles and it emerged that he had an address in Brighton.

The customs officers left the scene, convinced they had enough information to prove that there was more to the *Sea Mist* than met the eye. Back in their Cork office, frantic phone calls were made to check the backgrounds of the men with customs colleagues in their head office and with their equivalent in HM Customs in the UK. In Aghada the three men felt they had assuaged any suspicions held by the customs officers, but they could not have been more wrong. A tight net was falling not just around them but also around Richards, his teenage lover and her child.

The customs officers wanted to know where the skipper was staying. They carried out on-shore checks with taxi drivers to establish who had driven him to Cork city. They managed to track him down to Jurys Hotel, where officials conducted discreet enquiries with staff to establish what Richards was up to. They discovered a number of calls had been made to South America from the hotel. Another big discovery was made – it was only now that they became aware that a young woman and her child were also part of the mixed crew. They were staying with Richards in a room in the hotel.

By now, the investigators were convinced the *Sea Mist* had been used in a drug smuggling operation. Their counterparts in the HM Customs also had an interest in the vessel and believed it had been carrying drugs bound for the UK. At this point, officers thought the drugs had been off-loaded to another vessel, before it had pulled into what the crew had thought was a safe harbour.

The officers were not going to take a chance however, and decided to visit the ship again to carry out a full search. They notified Gardaí of their plans and two officers were designated to board the *Sea Mist* with the customs officials. It was planned to carry out the operation late that evening but the winds began to rise and the sea conditions became too dangerous. The team members were not concerned, as they knew the conditions would also hamper any plans the crew had to leave Aghada. Unknown to the crew, and the couple in Cork city, surveillance teams were watching both the boat and the hotel overnight to ensure none of the five adults left unnoticed.

Ironically, the operation was named '*Carinis*'. This was taken from the phrase '*Statio Bene Fide Carinis*', the Latin version of Cork city's motto, which is a 'safe harbour for all ships'. Officers had a feeling that Cork would not prove a safe harbour for the crew of the *Sea Mist*.

Early the following morning, the joint team got their operation underway, co-ordinated by Paddy O'Sullivan, who was the chief of Customs' Operations and Intelligence Unit. They boarded the vessel after 10.00am. The same three crew members were on board and the *Sea Mist* was moved to the Verolme dockyard in Cobh, as conditions in Aghada were too rough for a search. The men did not attempt to fight the boarding team, but efforts to move the vessel were initially hampered because the anchor got stuck in lobster pots. Eventually, the short voyage was underway. As the boat sailed towards Cobh, a mobile phone rang on board. Members of the boarding party listened as the first mate answered and told the caller that customs officers were on the *Sea Mist* and were going to search it. Checks of phone records later revealed that Richards made the phone call from the relative safety of Cork city.

The first mate's news terrified Richards. He knew it was time to leave Jurys Hotel and find somewhere else to stay. It certainly was not the right time to return to Aghada or go to Cobh. He walked around the city trying to find accommodation where he and his girlfriend could stay unnoticed for a while. He met a man on MacCurtain Street, who told him about a flat on Blarney Street in Cork's north inner city, which was available to rent. He felt this was the most viable option for them and the couple checked out of the hotel. The move came with its own hassles however – they had thought the hotel would be their base for the remainder of their short stay in Cork city and were expecting messages to come there for them. The only way out of that was to return to the hotel, later in the day, to check if the messages had arrived.

As the couple made themselves at home in their new accommodation, their crewmates were beginning to feel the heat in Cobh. Two customs officers on the team had received specialist training in Liverpool for rummaging ships suspected of being used for drug smuggling. They carried out a preliminary examination on board the *Sea Mist*. They were aiming to identify areas of the boat where drugs could have been concealed during the voyage from Venezuela. One area which aroused their suspicions was a spice rack in the galley area of the vessel. Shiny screws were holding the rack in place, at odds with the older appearance of screws in other areas of the ship. The rummage experts decided it was time to set about unscrewing the spice rack.

When the rack was pulled away, a dumb waiter shaft was unveiled and several packages could be seen stuffed into the cavity. The searchers were stunned. They had believed any drugs on board had been long off-loaded, but instead a provisional rummage led to the discovery of 100kg of cocaine. Wrapped in plastic, the packages were distinctive for reasons, other than the drugs they contained. Each was emblazoned with symbols of the ten of diamonds playing card. The word 'Diamentes' was also written on the packages.

When the drugs were discovered, the three crew members on board were arrested and taken away for questioning under new drug trafficking legislation. The Criminal Justice Drug Trafficking Act 1996 had just recently come into effect. It was part of a government crackdown on drugs crime following the deaths of Detective Garda Jerry McCabe and journalist Veronica Guerin in separate gun murders in June of that year.

In Cork city Gardaí were moving in on the remainder of the crew. They had maintained their surveillance on the hotel throughout the day. Da Silva Roy turned up that afternoon. They trailed her when she left the hotel and established that the couple and the child had moved to Blarney Street. Officers secured a search warrant and went back to the flat, where they arrested Richards that evening. Early the following morning, officers visited the flat again, this time to arrest his young girl-friend. Her toddler was placed into emergency care by the Southern Health Board, while she was taken for questioning.

The suspects could be held for up to seven days, benefiting the rummage team who felt there could be more drugs on board. Their search continued over three days and parts of the ship were dismantled to facilitate an in-depth probe of the vessel. During the intricate operation, it was kept under armed guard, hidden away from the curious eyes of the press and the public. The total amount of cocaine found weighed just over 599kg, with a purity of between 80 per cent and 85 per cent. The packages weighed a kilo or two kilos each, while some bales of heavier weights were also recovered on board.

After analysis at the State Laboratory in Dublin, a value of £47 million was put on the haul – the largest ever seizure of cocaine in the country up to then!

The huge haul came a month after the unrelated discovery of 38kg of the drug on board a cargo ship in Moneypoint, County Clare. The Singapore-registered *Front Guider* had sailed from Colombia and the drug was found in a secret compartment on board. The ship was carrying a legitimate cargo of 140,000 tonnes of coal for the nearby power station. Although the *Sea Mist* haul was believed to be destined for the UK, two seizures of the drug so close together was a wake up call for Irish authorities that there was now a burgeoning market for cocaine in Western Europe.

As the search was going on aboard the *Sea Mist*, naval navigation experts were brought in to examine the GPS navigation system and charts found on board, to determine the movements of the ship before it arrived in Cork harbour. The charts showed the *Sea Mist*'s route from Venezuela into Irish waters. The charts revealed that the vessel had made a stop-off in Trinidad on the way eastwards. Several cloth bags bearing the words: 'Trinidad and Tobago' were found on board. It was established that four people had been on board the vessel as it sailed from Venezuela, with an additional crew member coming onboard in Trinidad.

The DPP recommended that charges be brought against

the five adults, who had been on board the *Sea Mist* when it arrived into Cork harbour. He directed that the five should be charged with possession of cocaine for sale or supply to others, and with the unlawful importation of the drug into the State. The five were brought before a sitting of Cobh District Court on 1 October. Bail was refused because of the quantity of the seizure, the possible severity of the sentence if convicted, and that all five were foreign nationals with no connections to Ireland.

The arrival of the *Sea Mist* into Irish waters sparked off a huge international investigation by a team preparing a Book of Evidence for the trial. All five remained in custody, with da Silva Roy becoming increasingly anxious – due to her enforced separation from her son. The Venezuelan was being held in Limerick Prison, ahead of the trial. She was eagerly hoping that the trial would result in her release from prison and give her the freedom to once again look after her beloved son. She had been smitten by Richards, leading to her joining in the trip to Ireland. However, her decision to enter a relationship with such an older man lacked judgement – given that she was now facing trial for involvement in Ireland's largest cocaine seizure to date.

The case was due to come before Cork Circuit Criminal Court on 4 February the following year. However, da Silva Roy's legal team made attempts, two weeks beforehand, to have the charges against her struck out. In his application at Riverstown District Court in Midleton, da Silva Roy's solicitor said the young mum had been unaware there were drugs on the *Sea Mist* when she boarded the ship in Venezuela. Similar applications were made by solicitors representing two of the crew members. According to the *Cork Examiner*, one of the crew member's solicitor, Brian O'Herlihy, contended 'The evidence is that ... was merely an employee on the boat and unaware of the contraband on board.' He said there was nothing to link him to the drugs on board. However, their efforts were in vain and the State's case against the three remained in place. Judge John Clifford granted free legal aid for all five of the accused, allowing each of them access to a solicitor, barrister and senior counsel for the trial.

The opening of the case in Cork was expected to attract huge media interest for two reasons. The main one was that the seizure was the largest cocaine find in Ireland's history. Secondly, it was the first trial to get underway following the introduction of the Criminal Justice Drug Trafficking Act 1996.

When the case opened on 4 February skipper Gordon Richards decided to plead guilty to a charge of possession of cocaine for sale or supply during his arraignment. However, his four co-accused, including his girlfriend contested the charges all the way. Before evidence could be heard in the case, the presiding Judge AG Murphy made a ruling that angered the media. On 5 February he ruled that an embargo was being placed on all media reportage of the court proceedings until after the trial was finished. Judge Murphy explained his decision was made because a drugs trial had to be postponed the previous year because of an inaccurate media report. He said he had judicial discretion to make such an order and that the interests of the accused must be served first, the interests of justice be served next and the public interest thereafter. He added: 'The bar on publication in this case is not to hold the trial in camera. The doors are open, seats are available for people who want to come to court.'

The order incensed the local and national media. Applications by media outlets to have the order lifted failed and the case was taken to the High Court the following day. Leave was granted to RTÉ, The Irish Times Ltd, Independent Newspapers (Ireland) Ltd, Examiner Publications (Cork) Ltd, and News Group Newspapers Ltd to seek a judicial review of Judge Murphy's decision. Mr Justice Geoghegan said the applicants had an arguable case and gave leave for their case to be heard the following Monday, 10 February. The leave gave the media organisations permission to seek an order quashing the order of Judge Murphy. It also gave them leave to seek a declaration that they were entitled to publish, in accordance with law, true and accurate reports of the trials of the four accused. When the case was heard, the media's application was refused by Mr Justice Morris on 18 February. In his ruling, the judge said of Judge Murphy's decision: 'It seems to me that the learned trial judge must have had ample justification for his apprehension.'

The High Court decision did not deter the media. The five groups decided to challenge Mr Justice Morris's decision in the Supreme Court. However, the timing of the higher court's hearing was too late for them, as the trial they were fighting so hard to cover was continuing in Cork. Because the media was still fighting their battle, Judge Murphy's order stood and no coverage of the details emerging in court were being covered in the press or on broadcasts. However, the cocaine case was now a secondary feature for the media, because their challenge to the reporting embargo was about much more than wanting to cover this specific drugs importation case. The *Sea Mist* case had evolved into a fight for journalistic freedom. They were prepared to continue their battle in the Supreme Court the following November, even if the trial itself had been concluded.

The irony was that much of the trial could not have been reported, even if a ban had not been imposed. The jury of seven men and five women could not sit in the courtroom for great portions of the case, as legal argument dominated the proceedings. On 25 February the trial judge directed the jurors to find da Silva Roy not guilty of either charge. This was followed the next day by the acquittal of two of the crew members after a similar direction from Judge Murphy. The three were delighted. For the two crew members, it meant they were free to return to the lives they had before becoming involved in the misadventure on board the *Sea Mist*. For da Silva Roy, it was the key to renewing a normal maternal relationship with her son. As the trial of the first mate continued, she returned to her homeland, while her lover, Richards, remained in Ireland awaiting sentence.

Speaking to the *Cork Examiner*, outside the court after his acquittal, one of the crew members said: 'I am very happy, very relieved. I just want to try and get on with the rest of my life.' For his part, the other crew member admitted that he had felt anxious during the trial but he said that he was relieved with the judge's direction. He described the decision as 'justice at its best'.

While they were able to taste their first moments of freedom in four months, the first mate's future was uncertain. He had seen the acquittal of his three crewmates, but his own fate lay in the hands of the jury. Overnight, he worried about what would happen the following day. During the closing statement, he had heard the prosecution advise the jury that there was more than ample evidence to convict him. The first mate did not have too long to wait for a result. The jury was out for just two hours before returning to the courtroom in the Washington Street courthouse. When asked if they had come to a verdict, the foreman of the jury replied that they had found the defendant not guilty of either charge. The first mate sighed with relief at the outcome, delighted that he had been cleared of involvement with the bungled smuggling effort. Speaking after the verdict, he said he was very relieved and pleased to be found innocent. He added: 'The experience was a nightmare and I am glad it's over.'

He was not the only one who thought the trial had a nightmare quality. As it came to an end, the foreman of the jury expressed dissatisfaction with how they had been treated. The case had gotten underway on 5 February and the jury had spent most days out of the court until 25 February because of the legal argument, which had dominated the trial. The foreman said: 'All of the jury are wondering about expenses. We feel we have been treated disrespectfully. A lot of us are out of pocket quite a bit.' Judge Murphy replied: 'I have every sympathy, and no power to do anything about it. You are unlucky to be on a jury of this length. It is a specific duty that you have to perform and pay for. And there is nothing I can do about it.' He said juries got nothing except their lunch in Jurys Hotel every day, compared to 'in the mists of time' when members were paid five shillings. By early 2008 the same situation applied for jurors. Their employers were, however, obliged to pay them as usual.

Now that the trial was over, the spotlight moved back to Richards. Having seen the outcome of the case, the gravity of the situation sunk in. His young girlfriend had returned home. In contrast, he knew he was facing a substantial amount of time in prison. After all, he had pleaded guilty to involvement in the largest ever cocaine seizure in the Irish State. However, his legal team's efforts were not over.

Before the sentence was handed down, the court was told that Richards only became involved in the ill-fated smuggling mission when he was forced into it by 'evil men'. Richards's description of his entry into the world of drug smuggling was typical of couriers like him. He had hit bad times when he was enlisted in the operation, which was eventually to lead him into Cork harbour and the clutches of the Irish authorities. His background was in seafaring and he had been operating his own ferry business for tourists in the popular tourist area of St Martin, in Venezuela. However, his livelihood was destroyed when a hurricane hit the area in the mid 1990s, wrecking his boat and shattering his hopes for the business. It failed and Richards was in a state of financial chaos by the summer of 1996. The court heard that fate then took a hand in his situation when he was enlisted in a cocaine smuggling operation by men he met in Venezuela. He was ordered to take a cruiser trawler to Trinidad and on to

France, where he was to be given further instructions.

A statement made by Richards after his arrest was read out in court. In it, he said he was approached about the enterprise three months beforehand. He said the *Sea Mist* left the port city of Puerto de la Cruz, where da Silva Roy had an address. The statement continued that the *Sea Mist* was taken to Trinidad for repairs before the long journey to Ireland. The *Cork Examiner* related that he told how the drugs were loaded onto the vessel between Venezuela and Trinidad: 'An aeroplane dropped the shit off while we were at sea. I knew it was contraband and was pretty sure it was cocaine. I did not ask and I was not told.' He said he and another man hid the cocaine in the dumb waiter of the boat and that he had been promised a payment of $400,000 for his involvement in the operation.

The statement was not the only input heard from Richards in the court. He had decided to address the court directly, before his sentence was passed. He said: 'I have great remorse and shame for letting myself get involved in this. I got involved with some people who were very, very dangerous. I was pressured into this and I am sorry.'

He had also written a letter to Judge Murphy in a bid to win his sympathy before passing sentence. Richards told the judge that two armed South American men had threatened him and the safety of his teenage girlfriend and her child. The letter added: 'Something has to be done about these people. They are out of control. I won't be their last victim.'

However, Judge Murphy was not swayed by the emotive contributions from Richards and his legal team. He said he believed the massive payment was enough of a motivation for Richards to become involved in the cocaine smuggling plot. He rejected the notion that he had been an innocent person, who was preyed upon by dangerous, sinister and evil persons, who had forced him to take part. He said that if anyone was being coerced in the way Richards claimed, they should report the matter to police. He said that even if the skipper had been acting under duress, as he had claimed, it was not an acceptable excuse. The judge added that the cocaine was better named by its street term of 'White Death' and said the damage would have been incalculable if the shipment had made its way on to the market.

Judge Murphy wondered aloud what length of sentence he should impose on the *Sea Mist*'s captain. He said: 'What sentence is appropriate? Is fifty years too much? Is there any limit which society would consider appropriate? Probably not.' He speculated that a term of twenty-five to thirty years would be suitable punishment for the crime. However, he said he had to take the guilty plea into consideration, along with personal considerations. It had also emerged that international enquiries had shown that Richards had no previous conviction. Judge Murphy handed down a seventeen-year sentence to the devastated skipper. As his crewmates were getting used to their freedom, he was being led away by prison officers to serve his sentence.

Although the public's fascination with the arrival of the *Sea Mist* into Cork harbour stopped with the end of the trial, Richards was not finished with the Irish legal system. He and his defence team decided to take a challenge to the sentence in the Court of Criminal Appeal. At the time of sentencing, Richards was fifty-two-years-old. Even with remission of a quarter of his sentence, he would still be in his mid-sixties when his sentence was served. Spending that much time in prison at his age was daunting. His appeal was heard in the Four Courts, in Dublin, in November 1999. It failed. In passing judgement, Mr Justice Barron agreed that factors such as Richards's age and health concerns deserved consideration. The court had been told that the skipper was suffering from asthma because he was not able to adapt to the Irish climate. He had lived in South America for many years, although he had an address in Brighton. However, Mr Justice Barron ruled that the sentence was fair and would not be reduced.

As his sentence passed slowly, Richards occupied himself in prison with activities including woodwork. One of his handiworks was a scaled-down model of the *Sea Mist*. He caused no trouble while in prison and would, as a result, have automatically qualified for remission of four-and-a-quarter years off his sentence. He applied for full temporary release through the Irish parole board and was released in January 2008. He had not been due to be released until mid-2009. He left Ireland immediately to restart his life, now using the name John Earl Ewart. It had emerged during enquiries after his conviction that he was actually an American, with a false British passport under the name of Richards. He remained Richards in the Irish prison system, although his real name was also added to his file.

Shortly after his conviction the *Sea Mist* was sold off by the State. The vessel had been taken to Kilmacsimon boatyard, near Bandon after the seizure and was put up for sale following the trial in February 1997. In October of that year the ship fetched £20,606.53. The rib and a dory found with the vessel were sold off for £2,086.40.

The sale of the vessels came a month before the Supreme Court hearing on the media ban got underway. Although the trial was over by then, the media outlets wanted to ensure the court decisions taken by Judge Murphy and Mr Justice Morris did not set a precedent for coverage of other trials in the future. At the end of the two-day hearing, Chief Justice, Mr Liam Hamilton, said the five-judge court needed time to consider the challenge to the restrictions imposed by Judge Murphy. As a result, judgement was reserved in the case until the following April, when the court upheld the challenge taken by the media organisation. In its judgement, the Supreme Court ruled the media had been entitled to publish, in accordance with law, 'true and accurate' reports of the *Sea Mist* trial. It also ruled that Judge Murphy had given an order in excess of his jurisdiction. A ruling on costs was adjourned to July 1999, when the court granted costs to the media organisations. The undisclosed costs were paid by the State and divided equally between the five groups.

The Supreme Court decision should have been the end of a saga that had been sparked off by the unscheduled visit of the *Sea Mist* to Aghada. It had gone to trial quickly and the sale of the vessel had been completed almost a year after its arrival off the Cork coast. However, the arrests of the five crew members led to an international operation, which would lead to the downfall of one of the kingpins of the British drugs trade a decade later. The international operation would once again bring the *Sea Mist*'s first mate into a courtroom – this time in the UK.

Chapter 4

WRIGHT ORGANISATION

The decision to take the *Sea Mist* into Aghada was one gamble too many for the professional gambler behind the drug smuggling operation. Known as the Milkman, Brian Brendan Wright and his loyal lieutenants were eagerly awaiting the arrival of the vessel into British waters, when news emerged that the vessel had been detected by Irish authorities. Members of his international gang had already managed to safely land one cargo of cocaine onto UK soil, that year. The Wright organisation had been eagerly awaiting the latest consignment to meet the demands of their customers. However, the detention of the *Sea Mist* in Cobh meant that the Milkman had failed to deliver on this occasion.

The Dublin-born gambler and drug smuggler had moved to Cricklewood, in London, with his family when he was twelve-years-old. He was in trouble from an early age, spending time in a borstal as a teenager. When he reached adulthood, the world was changing and the use of illegal drugs was becoming increasingly popular. As the illegal trade grew, he began to see that it could offer him a viable income. He managed to build a drug smuggling empire that was managed by a network stretching from the UK across the Atlantic to the cocaine-producing stronghold of Colombia. However, his success in evading the authorities started to fade in 1996. As the five crew members of the *Sea Mist* were being questioned in Ireland, Brian Wright and his gang were counting their losses. A massive effort had been put into the *Sea Mist* project, with a plane dropping the consignment of cocaine onto the boat at sea, after the vessel had left Venezuela on its way to Trinidad and Tobago. Senior members of the gang had travelled to the Caribbean from the UK to meet the *Sea Mist* en route and ensure all was well with the consignment before it left for Europe. Although the *Sea Mist* capture was a big dent to Wright's profit margins, his operation was large enough to be able to sustain it.

As the final motions were being put in place for the *Sea Mist*'s voyage, a yacht called the *Casita* was being steered towards the south coast of England by American Jim Goodrich and Canadian Alain Deland. The two men had started out from St Maarten, in the Caribbean, in June with a cargo of 600kg of cocaine. Arriving safely at coordinates at sea close to the harbour town of Poole, the men's yacht was met by another boat, the *Selina*. Wright's most trusted operator Kevin Hanley and associate Judith Parks were on board. The precious cargo was off-loaded onto the *Selina* and whisked into England – without being noticed. Coopering – the method of transferring cargo from one vessel to another – was a method used frequently by Wright's gang. It allowed drugs to be transferred to a local-registered vessel, thus avoiding the suspicion which could surround the arrival of foreign-registered ships.

Now that the *Casita* was safely unloaded, there was nothing left for Deland and Goodrich to do but await the arrival of the *Sea Mist* into British waters. The removal of the cocaine from the *Sea Mist* into their yacht for delivery to the Wright gang was to be their responsibility. The nearby port of Lymington looked a good place to while away the weeks until then. As late August arrived, the duo left the port town and travelled westwards to meet with the *Sea Mist*. However, their plans were scuppered when news came through of the Irish authorities' capture – then they knew there was no point in waiting around. The *Sea Mist* would not be heading towards Britain in the coming weeks and it was time for Deland and Goodrich to return to the US.

Even though the *Sea Mist* seizure was a heavy blow to Wright, he firmly believed that it was a hurdle he and his team could overcome. There was plenty more cocaine in South America to replace what had been lost, and a ready market to help make up for the loss of revenue from the seized consignment. As far as he was aware, there was nothing to connect him with the *Sea Mist* and his profit-making operation could continue as if the Cobh seizure had never happened.

However, a search of the vessel in Cobh led to the discovery of enough clues to link the Wright organisation to the consignment. Key documents, including a photocopy of a passport belonging to Judith Parks, had been found on board. The information was passed on by Irish customs to their counterparts in the UK. Mobile phones belonging to an associate of Wright were also found on board. After the February 1997 sentencing of the skipper, then known as Gordon Richards, a fuller picture of the operation behind the Cobh seizure began to emerge. Among the new information was that Richards was in fact an American called John Earl Ewart. As the Irish authorities' 'Operation Carinis' evolved into the international investigation codenamed 'Operation Extend', it was felt that Ewart could prove a vital cog in the efforts to bring Brian Wright and his team to justice for their drug smuggling operation.

On the other side of the Irish Sea, investigators in the UK set up a massive surveillance operation to identify Wright's key associates. For a man so heavily involved in the horse racing world, it was not surprising that they included friends from that scene. Other close allies were former son-in-law Paul Shannon, friend Ian Kiernan and Wright's beloved son Brian Anthony Wright.

When the surveillance team identified Kevin Hanley as a key member of Wright's loyal group, they struck it lucky. He was one of the most vital cogs in the drug smuggling empire, but had been unknown to the authorities before the surveillance operation kicked off. As the *Casita* episode showed, Hanley was involved in the transportation aspect of the operation and also had responsibility for distributing the newly-imported cocaine to markets within the UK. When the British authorities nabbed him in late 1998, Wright knew the game was very close to the end for him and his gang.

Hanley had been under surveillance in the autumn of 1998 when contacts from South America arrived in London to meet members of the Wright organisation, including him. The visitors included Brazilian economist Ronald Soares. He was a link between Wright's gang and drug cartels in Colombia. The HM Customs surveillance operation on meetings between the English gang members and their visitors established that the Wright organisation had not learned from the mistakes of the *Sea Mist*. Officers learned that other drug smuggling operations were planned for the following year, with the destinations including the UK, Australia and the US. The surveillance operation also taught them that Wright's network had successfully organised shipments into Britain in 1998 as well.

The year was not over yet and the authorities were keen to

make a big swoop on the gang. The visitors returned to South America as Hanley, Wright and their associates continued with their operation. Unknown to Hanley, the authorities were closing in on him and he was arrested in the early hours of a November morning while driving in London. He was shocked when members of the Metropolitan Police stopped his car and carried out a search. They were acting on an anonymous tip-off and the informant's knowledge was impeccable. When the boot was opened, 29kg of cocaine were found. The haul was worth stg£1.5 million. With Hanley's arrest came the biggest blow for Wright. The amount of cocaine was only a tiny fraction of the *Sea Mist* seizure, but the significance of Hanley's detention was huge because of his key role in the organisation.

The development was deemed so disastrous that Soares returned to the UK to have a face-to-face meeting with Wright. This would have been unheard of before Hanley's arrest, but the middle man was now in custody and Wright had to take back the reins of the operation. Soares's visit was sparked by the need to do a spot check of the cocaine left unsold in Britain, which had been shipped from South America. With Hanley now out of the distribution scene, it was time to examine how much the gang owed their South American suppliers. Wright reached an agreement with Soares that the cocaine which lay undistributed by Hanley would now come under Soares's control. He realised that it was time to scale down operations in the UK. Hanley's arrest was proof that the customs' spotlight was now firmly on his organisation. He also felt it was an opportune time to flee to the safety of his villa in Spain, until the heat died down.

Soares remained in the UK and met regularly with two men, Barry Fennell and Roger Newton. Newton was a friend he had met while the Englishman was in South America. Fennell was an associate of Brian Wright and Kevin Hanley. During his time in England, the South American spent some time at Newton's home in Leigh-on-Sea, near Southend. In February 1999, almost two months after his arrival, he began taking possession of the consignment, which had been under Hanley's care. Cocaine stored in a farm in Laleham, in Middlesex, was transferred to a lock-up garage in Leigh-on-Sea, under the agreement reached by Soares with Wright after Hanley's arrest. The operation was under surveillance by customs officers, who decided it was time to move in on Soares, Newton, Fennell and other associates – before the gang went their separate ways. There was the possibility that some would leave the jurisdiction, if the authorities did not act now. Officers went to the farm and the garage, and recovered a combined total of 472kg of cocaine, worth stg£61 million.

Several arrests were made and among those taken into custody were Soares, Brian Anthony Wright, Newton, Fennell and a Colombian student called Liliana Uribe. The young woman was studying in London and had been seen meeting Soares and another Brazilian associate during their stay in Britain. When she was arrested, she was found in possession of $127,000 and stg£90,000. She was questioned on suspicion of being involved in money laundering for Wright's operation.

Although major figures had been arrested, including Wright Junior, the central figure in the organisation was still at large. The Milkman had left for Spain at the perfect time. However, the authorities were still keen to capture him and an international arrest warrant was issued for him. His homes in Chelsea and Frimley were both raided, causing him to get nervous. It was time to move again and he made plans for his escape from his Spanish hideout. He arranged for a private jet to fly from Stansted airport to the Sierra Nevada Mountains in Spain. The plane picked up the drugs tycoon there and flew him to Bodrum in Turkey. From there, he fled to the Turkish republic of Northern Cyprus, which had no extradition treaty with the UK. He knew that even if he was tracked down, the UK authorities could not force him back to Britain.

Arrest warrants were also issued for a man called Godfried Hoppenbrouwers and another man. Hoppenbrouwers, who lived in Brazil, was a known associate of Kevin Hanley. He owned one yacht called the *Cyan* in which cocaine was found, resulting in a conviction, and had also purchased the *Selina* with Kevin Hanley for coopering drugs off the English coast.

Back in the UK, the authorities prepared for the trials of those who had been arrested there. As with any major drug trafficking investigation, enquiries were also made internationally to help build a case. Investigators decided it was time to see how helpful Ewart could be – they met with him in prison in Ireland. Safe in the knowledge that he was serving one of the longest Irish prison sentences for drug trafficking, Ewart decided to co-operate and outlined the operation behind the smuggling effort he had been involved in. Interviews with him provided investigators with a broader picture of a network which extended from Colombia, Mexico, Venezuela, Brazil and Panama to the Caribbean, Europe and South Africa.

Enquiries identified the use of a number of key yachts used in the smuggling empire of Wright, including the *Casita*. Investigations established that another yacht called the *Moonstreak* had arrived into the UK in 1997 with a cargo of approximately 300kg of cocaine.

The arrival of another yacht the following year raised the name of the first mate who had featured in the trial resulting from the *Sea Mist* seizure. He owned the vessel whose name was changed in 1998. Enquiries revealed that the newly-named boat had sailed from Trinidad and Tobago that summer, arriving in Salcombe Harbour on the south coast of England in September. It was carrying a consignment of 400kg of cocaine.

Customs officials decided to place him under surveillance after the discovery of his yacht. As a result of the operation, he was arrested in London in March 1999. When arrested, he was trying to access a cash deposit box that was found to be holding almost £300,000. A further £75,000 was found at a flat he was renting. As he awaited trial, he could not believe he was back in the same situation again, just two years after being acquitted in Cork. However, a six-week trial at Bristol Crown Court in May 2001 had the same result and his concerns were unfounded. He was acquitted by a jury.

Among those brought to trial after him was another sailor, Paul Rodgers. He had crewed the *Moonstreak* in 1997 from St Vincent, in the West Indies, to Lymington, on the south coast of England. Investigators had also established that he had met with Soares during his visit to London in autumn 1998. Rodgers was arrested in August 1999 and went on trial in Woolwich Crown Court in May 2000. His case was one of eleven involving the Wright gang to come before the court that month. After a fourteen-month trial, he was found guilty of importation in July 2001 and was given a sixteen-year sentence.

The remainder included Soares, Wright Junior, Kiernan

and Shannon. They all pleaded not guilty to the charges facing them. Among the witnesses giving evidence were maritime experts who had examined the voyages undertaken by the yachts at the heart of the operation. Their evidence brought a novel dimension to the proceedings as their investigation included examination of GPS systems used by the Wright organisation. Such systems were new in the maritime world, highlighting the use of the most up-to-date equipment by the gang. Telephone contacts between the suspects had also been analysed and was used in evidence, including contact from the UK to other parts of the world. Some of the accused had been found in possession of address books with contact details for associates, which helped experts to trace them during analysis of phone records. During the trial, evidence was heard from some witnesses that Brian Brendan Wright was in Northern Cyprus.

As with Rodgers, the trials of the other ten defendants ended after fourteen months. The case was the longest customs trial in the UK. It was the second longest in British criminal history. The gang was dealt a severe blow with the verdicts in the trial. Soares was found guilty of importation conspiracy dating back to 1996 and 1997. The Brazilian economist was given a twenty-four-year sentence. Four others were also found guilty, including Wright's son Brian Junior. He was found guilty of importation in 1996 and was given sixteen years in prison. Wright's ex-son-in-law, Paul Shannon, was handed down five years for conspiracy to supply drugs. Kiernan was found guilty of importation and given twenty years for his role.

Uribe, Newton, Fennell and Hanley had also been due to go on trial but they each decided to plead guilty to their charges. Uribe was sentenced to two-and-a-half years for money laundering. Newton was given a nine-year sentence for possessing drugs with intent to supply. Fennell was handed down a ten-year sentence for importation. Hanley had been charged with importation and conspiracy to supply cocaine. He got a fifteen-year sentence, bringing the total of sentences meted out in the trials to 120.5 years. Two of the eleven facing trial were found not guilty. In summing up, the judge said it was estimated that at least 3 tonnes of cocaine were imported into the UK between 1996 and 1998, the focus of the 'Extend' enquiry.

Hanley's downfall was helped enormously by the capture of Goodrich and Deland in the US. The duo had left the west coast of England after the capture of the *Sea Mist* and life went on as normal for them, on the other side of the Atlantic, as the Irish and British authorities began their clampdown on the Wright gang. However, the men's good fortune was not to last. They were arrested in May 1998 when attempting to smuggle 2 tonnes of cocaine into Fort Lauderdale in Florida. Goodrich was sentenced to eighteen years for his part in the botched effort, while his colleague was jailed for thirteen years. Investigations had revealed their link to the Wright organisation and US customs notified their British counterparts in December 1999 of their coup in convicting the two men.

The US convictions were a further boost to the British authorities. Having enlisted the aid of the *Sea Mist* skipper, they knew that Goodrich and Deland could also play vital roles in the attempt to smash Wright's drug smuggling ring. Goodrich agreed to become a prosecution witness and told them of the coopering of the *Casita* to the *Selina* in the waters off Britain. Central to this evidence was his assertion of Hanley's involvement in the operation, and the presence of Judith Parks on board.

By now, the net was also closing in on Parks and Hanley's associate, Hoppenbrouwers. An arrest warrant was still in existence for him. The failed Fort Lauderdale operation had now brought him back into the frame. In February 2000 he was arrested in Miami and was charged with money laundering and drug offences related to the Fort Lauderdale incident. Efforts to have him extradited back to the UK, on foot of the international arrest warrant, failed because of the US proceedings.

As he awaited trial, international enquiries were on-going in a joint operation between the Irish, British and US authorities. Part of the attention was being focused on Parks. Investigations after the *Sea Mist* seizure had identified the Englishwoman as another key figure in the overall Wright gang. She was arrested in the American Virgin Islands in August 2001 and charged with drug offences. She pleaded guilty and was sentenced to eight years in prison.

After her decision to plead guilty, the investigators believed she also had information that could help them advance their case against Hoppenbrouwers and the remainder of the Wright gang. When they approached her to ask for her co-operation she agreed. She confirmed she had been on board the *Selina* in the summer of 1996, when it coopered the *Casita*, and that she had been paid stg£35,000 for her role in that job. She gave details of coopering consignments in 1998 from three vessels on another boat, with Hoppenbrouwers and a South African man called Hilton Van Staden. The cocaine was taken to a safe house for storage and then taken away by Hanley. Again, she got stg£35,000 before returning to the US. Irish customs officers Paddy O'Sullivan and Dick Beamish travelled to Miami to give evidence in the trial in relation to evidence from the *Sea Mist* investigation. Testimony given by Parks, the Irish customs officers and their counterparts from the UK resulted in Hoppenbrouwers being found guilty. He was convicted and sentenced to thirty years in prison.

Parks was also to play a role in the conviction of Van Staden. He had been arrested in March 2000 in similar circumstances as the first mate from the *Sea Mist*, when he went to access a safe deposit box in London. The box held stg£490,000 in cash. He was a known associate of Hoppenbrouwers and had an address in Savannah, in the US. He was an accomplished sailor. Parks said Van Staden had paid her for her role in coopering. His trial for drug offences got underway in September 2001 at Bristol Crown Court, but a re-trial was ordered when the jury could not come to a verdict. He was brought to trial again in June 2002 and pleaded guilty to importation of drugs. He was sentenced to nine years in prison.

By now, fifteen people around the world had been convicted as part of the crackdown on Brian Wright Senior and his associates. He, however, was still at large.

A BBC *Panorama* programme entitled *The Corruption of Racing* was aired in October 2002 and identified Wright as being involved in race fixing. The programme had access to files belonging to the Jockey Club, courtesy of the club's former head of security, Roger Buffham. He told the programme that Wright had corrupted a generation of jockeys racing in Britain. Allegations were also made by ex-jockey and trainer Dermot Browne. He said he and other jockeys had been offered cash, cocaine and prostitutes to fix races for Brian Wright. Browne also claimed he had helped dope twenty-three horses at Wright's request in 1990. Browne had been already 'warned off' for ten years in 1992, after being found guilty of several separate offences. He was banned for a further twenty years in November 2002 after the Wright revelations.

As the name of Brian Brendan Wright became a by-word for scandal in the racing world – the man himself was still lying low in Northern Cyprus. Although he had been tracked down by the Panorama team, he didn't leave. He was safe in the knowledge of the lack of powers that the British authorities had over him, while he lived there. However, by September 2003 he felt it was time to leave and returned to Spain from his hideout. News of his return quickly reached the British authorities and they put a plan in motion to have him brought to justice. Wright was arrested in Spain in March 2005, on foot of a European arrest warrant, and taken back to Britain to face trial.

Once more, the input of witnesses from the US proved a major advantage to the British authorities. Four prosecution witnesses from the US were called to provide assistance in the case against Wright. Goodrich and Parks co-operated again. Also on board were Hoppenbrouwers and a man called Alex de Cubas. As with Hoppenbrouwers, de Cubas was serving a thirty-year sentence in the US. He had been given the sentence for his role in the South American side of the operation. He and the other three prosecution witnesses were given a grant of immunity from prosecution in the UK under the Serious Organised Crime and Police Act 2005. This was the first time the Act was used in a case.

With the help of their evidence, sixty-year-old Wright was found guilty of two charges by a majority jury in April 2007. The verdict came after a two-month trial at Woolwich Crown Court. The charges were conspiracy to evade the prohibition and importation of a controlled drug, and conspiracy to supply drugs. Comedian Jim Davidson was a character witness in the trial. Davidson at the time had asked Wright to be godfather to his son. The two men had met at a race meeting in Kempton, more than twenty years earlier. After his conviction, Wright told Judge Peter Moss that there were no mitigating factors to be taken into account when considering a sentence. Judge Moss adjourned the case until the following day, to allow him to read health reports on Wright before sentencing him. The Milkman suffered from a heart complaint and had a pacemaker fitted in 2006. Addressing the judge, Wright's counsel, Jerome Lynch QC, said: 'He knows, as does his family that he will probably die in jail.'

At the sentencing on 3 April, the drug lord was given a thirty-year sentence. Judge Peter Moss was quoted in *The Irish Times* as saying to Mr Wright: 'You were able to live a lavish lifestyle here in the UK and in your villa in Spain, disguising the true origin of your wealth behind your apparent success as a gambler. You were a master criminal, manipulative, influential. I accept you will be a very much older man when you will be entitled to release. I accept too the possibility that you may not live that long.

Nevertheless, those who import and distribute call upon themselves lengthy terms of imprisonment. You played for the highest stakes and won, for a number of years, a luxury lifestyle. You well knew the consequences of detection and conviction.'

Three other people had also been scheduled to stand trial with him. However, they pleaded guilty in advance of it. Anni Rowland, from Oxfordshire, pleaded guilty to conspiracy to supplying drugs and money laundering. Brian Coldwell, from Notting Hill Gate, and Gary Mace, from Moreton-in-the-Marsh, in Gloucestershire, both offered guilty pleas to money laundering charges.

The conviction and sentencing of Wright was the end of an eleven-year investigation extending from Ireland and Britain to the US, South America and the Caribbean. The result was a massive coup for the authorities involved and the capture of Wright was ample reward for the efforts put into smashing his organisation.At the end of his trial, Director of Criminal Investigations for HM Revenue and Customs, Roy Clark, said: 'Operation Extend has been an investigation without parallel in UK drugs law enforcement. UK customs investigators, working hand-in-hand with their counterparts in the United States, have dismantled probably the most sophisticated and successful global cocaine trafficking organisation ever to target the UK. This has resulted in successful prosecutions at all levels of the conspiracy, from the Colombian suppliers, to the transporters, to the members of the UK distribution network and ultimately brought the head of that network, Brian Brendan Wright, to justice.'Twenty people were convicted in Ireland, Britain and the US in connection with the Wright organisation.

With the criminal proceedings out of the way, the next step was to target the massive profits that the Wright organisation had accumulated through their drug trade. In May 2004 *Underworld Rich List*, a BBC3 programme, named Wright as the richest British drug baron. He was then estimated to be worth at least stg£100 million. In April 2008 Judge Peter Moss directed Brian Wright to pay a confiscation order of stg£2,311,371 at a hearing in Woolwich Crown Court. The judge said Wright would have to serve a consecutive ten-year sentence if the money is not paid within twelve months. Speaking after the case, Robert Alder of HM Revenue and Customs' Restraint and Confiscation Unit said: 'The size of this confiscation order reflects Brian Brendan Wright's role at the very top of a global organised crime network that lived off the misery of the countless victims of the illegal drugs trade. Confiscation orders like this ensure that career criminals, such as Wright, are denied the opportunity to profit from their crimes.'

Wright had managed to escape the authorities for eleven years after the *Sea Mist*'s capture. However, his luck ran out when he took the gamble of leaving Northern Cyprus.

Chapter 5

BRIME

As the phone rang out, Inspector Jim Fitzgerald had to think fast. The call had not been expected and the way he dealt with it would be the difference between success and failure for him and his team.

The phone was not his own. It had been seized in a Garda operation on the Ring of Kerry in recent days. The operation followed the arrival of a suspect fishing boat called *Gerry's 1* in the harbour of Ballinskelligs on 10 July 1993. The boat was new to the area and aroused the suspicions of local people. However, an alert had been made about the half-decker as it had already been spotted in an unusual anchorage, west of Kenmare, by a coastal contact. He had informed customs officers and Gardaí about its presence. Investigations revealed the *Gerry's 1* had come from Wales to Ballinskelligs. After its arrival in the South Kerry harbour, a decision was taken by the authorities to board it. Gardaí went onto the vessel and met one man on board. A second crew member had gone to a local garage to purchase a part for the boat's engine. When he arrived back to the boat, he was surprised to find they had visitors. Two Welshmen were searched and both were arrested, after a small quantity of cannabis was found. They were later released from custody on bail. He had been charged with possession of the cannabis, which was enough to make a small number of joints. He disappeared before the case came to court.

However, the *Gerry's 1* was not the only reason for suspicion. The focus had been broadened to also consider a white car, which was regularly seen arriving into Ballinskelligs to rendezvous with the two men, who had been on board the *Gerry's 1*. Gardaí put the car under surveillance and as a result, moved in to arrest two men in Ballinskelligs on the same day. They were in the area with two women, one of whom had a young child. Local officers did not know the men but checks on them led to the identity of oneof them being revealed as David Huck. The two British men were living in the Killaloe area of Clare, but authorities in the UK advised Gardaí that David Huck was considered a major player in the international drugs trade.

David Huck's presence in the area and the connection to the crew of the half-decker led Gardaí to believe there was a shipment of drugs somewhere off the coast of Ireland. This was underlined by a call received by customs from their counterparts in the UK. Intelligence had been received that a vessel was heading northwards from Africa, believed to be laden with cannabis. HM Customs had no idea of the vessel's location but had notified their Irish counterparts in the hope that they could locate the boat between them. Gardaí notified the navy and the air corps, and a naval vessel and a helicopter were dispatched off the southwest coast, to establish if a suspect ship was hanging around waiting to rendezvous with the *Gerry's 1*. Time was running out as officers in Kerry only had twelve hours to question the two men. A further difficulty facing the crew of the naval vessel and the helicopter was that a boat race was also passing through the area, arriving in Kerry from Dublin, making it more difficult to determine if there was a suspicious vessel in the area.

The air and sea trawl did not establish the presence of any suspect boat and the two men were released without charge. However, Gardaí decided to confiscate the mobile phones that the men had in their possession. At that time, mobile phones were rare. The men's phones had been rented in Dublin, and Gardaí suspected they were being used to keep in touch with contacts at sea. The handsets were kept in Cahersiveen Garda station, where they were charged to keep their batteries alive. The possibility of Huck's associates calling the phones was not considered at that stage. The authorities felt there was still a possibility that a drugs run could be brought into Kerry and surveillance was continued in the areas off

Valentia Island, Ballinskelligs and Portmagee, over the next two days.

The naval vessel, the *LE Orla*, had been patrolling the west coast in search of any suspect vessel, under Lieutenant Commander Mark Mellet. With no confirmation that the *Gerry's 1* was planning to meet another boat, the crew on board the naval vessel was at a disadvantage. On the evening of 12 July it was decided to drop anchor in a quiet area, to give the crew on board a chance to rest and prepare for any possible action in the coming days. The *LE Orla* was off the coast of West Cork, at that stage, and it pulled into Long Island Sound, near Schull. Not wanting to raise the suspicions of any other vessels in the area, the crew blacked out the ship by turning off all lights on board. They then settled in to rest for the night.

However, by now things were beginning to fall into place for the authorities. As the crew on the *LE Orla* were dropping anchor off West Cork, Inspector Fitzgerald left the station in Cahersiveen to return home to Tralee. As he was leaving, he spotted the two phones and decided to take one away with him. He was not even sure why he picked up the phone but as he made his way towards Tralee, it began to ring. The time was 8.40pm. A man called Gerry was on the other end of the line and was not sure whether the man receiving his call was to be trusted. In his Dublin accent, he asked the Inspector where another man called David was. Knowing he had to be unflinching in his replies, Inspector Fitzgerald quickly replied, in a falsified English accent, that David was in Dublin. Gerry made it clear that he wanted to speak to David, so the officer promised he would make every effort to track him down by the time of his next call.

Before ending the call, the Inspector decided to ask where Gerry was now located. He knew the call was coming from a location off the Irish coast and Gerry confirmed this by giving him coordinates for a point at sea. Inspector Fitzgerald called to Tralee Garda station, where he and a colleague established from maps that Gerry had called from close to Loop Head. By now, it was clear to Inspector Fitzgerald, and the rest of the Gardaí and customs officers on the case, that Gerry and his fellow crew were waiting at sea to drop off a consignment of drugs to another smaller vessel.

Gerry was getting frustrated by the absence of a boat to hook up with his vessel. In the call to the Inspector, he demanded, 'Where the fucking hell are you? We're waiting for the last two days.' He said morale on board was low, the mainsail was broken and water was running out. He added that the crew did not want to be hanging around at sea and that it was the last chance of getting the 'stuff' off. The crew members were so close to the end of their tether that threats were made to throw the cargo overboard – if arrangements could not be made to off-load it. With the crew's patience running out,

Inspector Fitzgerald knew they had to be reassured and he said he was doing his best to make arrangements for a rendezvous at sea. As far as Gerry was aware, the man at the other end of the phone could be trusted. Unknown to him however, Inspector Fitzgerald was the man tasked in the Kerry Garda division with responsibility for drugs law enforcement.

Gerry's call to the phone, confiscated from David Huck, was further confirmation that the fishing vessel was linked to drug smuggling. Customs and Gardaí were now convinced that the fishing boat in Ballinskelligs was supposed to have linked up with a mother ship at sea but plans had to be abandoned because of engine trouble and poor weather conditions. Gerry's frustration had convinced them that the mother ship was still lingering at sea, with a cargo that should have been transferred to the smaller boat. It was time to contact the navy and task a crew to investigate.

Lieutenant Commander Mellet was preparing to go to bed for the night at around 11.30pm but listened first to the weather forecast for the following day. He heard a crackle of communication come through the radio system, from the naval base, and guessed there was news in relation to the *Gerry's 1* operation. The crew on the naval vessel was told there was reason to believe that there was something suspicious afoot off the Clare coast. With plans for rest abandoned, the crew headed northwards. Among them was a Garda Sergeant, Christopher

McCarthy, who regularly travelled out on naval vessels during salmon poaching patrols. The Dublin-based officer had also worked in the drugs enforcement area, which was opportune given the operation that was now underway.

At that time, the navy had developed an operational tactic, aimed at ensuring the element of surprise, to help them in targeting vessels carrying contraband. If the crew on board suspect vessels were given only short notice of the presence of a naval ship in the area, they would have too little time to throw any contraband overboard. As the *LE Orla* left the safety of Long Island Sound, the forty-two-member crew knew time was of the essence in this operation, if they were to make it to the Clare coast before daylight dawned at 5.10am. With more than 160km ahead of them, calculations told them they would make it with just about twenty minutes to spare before dawn. During the journey northwards, much planning took place on board, to ensure the maximum safety of all those involved in the operation. A primary boarding party, led by Lieutenant Declan Fleming, was selected. If a suspect vessel was in the area, the team would leave the naval vessel on a rib and head towards the other boat to investigate it. A back-up crew for a second rib was also chosen. Above all, the aim was to identify the suspect vessel and move in on it before giving its crew a chance to realise the *LE Orla* was in the area.

During the trip northwards, the crew on the naval vessel

was determined that the navy's presence in the seas, off the west coast, should not be noticed by fishing vessels. Salmon season was underway and there were a number of fishermen working off the coast that morning, even though it was pitch dark. Officers were worried that some fishermen would comment about the presence of the navy over the radio communication system, thereby unconsciously tipping off any suspect vessel in the area. So as not to arouse suspicion, lighting on the *LE Orla* was arranged to make it appear like a fishing vessel. The move seemed to work, as nobody commented on it over the radio system. Further information was being fed through from the naval base and the crew were told that the vessel they were looking for was a ketch located in the waters near Loop Head.

A check on the radar system showed a vessel moving southwards, as the *LE Orla* pulled close to Loop Head. There was a heavy mist and a troubled sea. Winds blowing from the southwest meant that conditions were not favouring the smaller boat. Feeling confident that it was the ketch they were looking for, the first boarding party was dispatched in its rib to investigate. With no way of knowing if the crew on the other vessel was armed, the *LE Orla* proceeded quickly in the wake of the rib – to ensure the men on board had back-up if things turned nasty. By now, it was around 5.00am with literally minutes to go before dawn.

The preliminary investigation revealed that the vessel was

indeed a ketch, called the *Brime*. The 19m vessel was 11km from the Irish coast. As a result, it could be legally detained in the 19-km limit. The arrival of the navy so close to the *Brime* caused consternation on board. Feeling cornered, the crew decided to fight the visitors and attempted to ram the boarding party. An effort was also made to scuttle the *Brime* but it failed. The boarding party managed to make it on to the ketch safely and they knew they had to act quickly to ensure they were not over-powered by the four-man crew. They were also fearful that the vessel could be booby-trapped after the earlier attempt to scuttle it.

By that point, three of the four crew members had dashed below deck to escape the boarding party. They were terrified of their visitors. According to the *Cork Examiner,* the skipper of the vessel, Egbertus Marius Van Onzen, later said: 'I did not recognise the personnel as naval. It could have been the Mafia.' However, the crew quickly realised that the navy were on board and efforts were made to sink the vessel – by opening a valve to let seawater in. With the navy present, the men would not be left to drown, so their lives were not in danger. Sinking the vessel could be the best way to get rid of the contraband on board. By now, back-up from the *LE Orla* had arrived on the ketch and naval engineers managed to stem the flow of water through the opened valve.

Van Onzen and his three crew mates – Gerry Fitzgerald,

Wayne Bland and Frank Loopmans – were apprehended and their hands and feet were bound by the boarding party. This was done partly to ensure the crew could easily be lifted off the ketch, if it transpired that it was booby-trapped. Sergeant McCarthy arrested the four men and the vessel was searched. Suspect packets were stored in every available area of the boat and the boarding party was jubilant. The officers believed they had scuppered a major drug smuggling effort, and decided to sail the *Brime* into Fenit for a more in-depth search.

Heavy rain was falling as the ketch was brought into the Kerry port. When the boarding party arrived with their prize, Gardaí greeted them on the pier and took the four men into custody. They were brought to Tralee Garda station for questioning, as attention was focused in Fenit on removing the suspect packets – two tonnes in all – from the Guernsey-registered *Brime*. The ketch had been registered in the Channel Islands under a company name. Closer examination was later to reveal that the vessel actually belonged to David Huck.

The seizure came just two months after the seizure of 150kg of cannabis buried in sand at the Warren beach in Rosscarbery, and the discovery of hauls in Tragumna, near Skibbereen, totalling almost 700kg of cannabis resin, within a week of each other that year.

Removing the packets of suspected cannabis resin from the *Brime* was a big job. The harbour was sealed off as the operation got underway. Seventy-one packets of the drug were removed, each weighing about 25kg. Eight holdalls containing the drug were also removed. The haul was loaded into a van for transportation to Dublin for analysis. The examination of the haul would help determine the exact value of the haul, later to be placed at £19.5 million. The removal of the cannabis was carried out under the watchful eye of Sergeant Eugene O'Sullivan, who was in charge of preserving the scene. The Ballyheigue-based sergeant accompanied the consignment to Dublin, with the van driver and Garda John Evans from Tralee Garda station, in the early hours of the following morning, under armed escort.

Back in Tralee, the four crew members of the *Brime* were frustrated by developments. Each of them had become involved in the venture for the money they would receive at the end and could not believe their misfortune. They had never intended to come in to Ireland, but their plans had changed dramatically after the fishing vessel was forced into Ballinskelligs. They were angry that they were the fall guys for the failed venture – while those behind the operation got away.

Nevertheless, they had committed an offence by bringing their cargo within the 19-km radius of Ireland and a decision was taken to charge all four in connection with the seizure. From early on, Wayne Bland outlined his role in the operation and Gerry Fitzgerald also took responsibility for his part. However, Van Onzen and Loopmans decided to fight the charges of importation and possession, including possession with the intent of sale or supply.

As the Book of Evidence for the case was being prepared, the ketch was removed to the naval base in Haulbowline. It took more than a day to sail the vessel to the Cork base, where it would remain docked until the case was completed. The seas were very high during the voyage. Once the vessel arrived safely into Haulbowline, it remained there indefinitely. Its future would be determined in court at the conclusion of the trial. The seizure was a huge coup for Irish law enforcers. In the Dáil, then Minister for Justice, Máire Geoghegan Quinn, said the seizure was destined for Milford Haven in Wales.

When the case came to trial on 2 March 1994, only Van Onzen from Amsterdam, the Netherlands and Loopmans of Antwerp, Belgium went before the jury. Bland and Fitzgerald had both pleaded guilty to the unlawful possession of cannabis resin for the purpose of supplying to another, and being in unlawful possession of the drug. They were remanded in ongoing custody while the trial of their crew mates went ahead. The case was heard by Judge Kevin O'Higgins and a jury of eight men and four women. The two faced six charges each – two counts of unlawfully importing cannabis resin within the territorial seas of the State; possession of cannabis resin for the purpose of unlawfully supplying it to another, and being in the unlawful possession of cannabis resin, on 12 and 13 July. An interpreter was used to translate the court proceedings for the accused.

In opening the State's case, counsel Denis Vaughan Buckley said there would be an abundance of evidence to find the accused guilty on all counts. He said: 'It must have been one of the largest amounts of drugs ever found in this country. It was enormous.' Evidence was heard from Gardaí and naval personnel throughout the trial relating to the different areas of investigation in the run up to the capture of the *Brime* and its aftermath. Lieutenant Commander Mark Mellet said that at 5.05am on 13 July, the *Brime* was 7km inside the 19-km zone. The court heard that when Van Onzen was charged with importation on 13 July, he said: 'I did not want to bring it into Ireland. I never had the intention of importing it into Ireland.' To the charges of possession and the other charges, he had replied, 'It's true.'

Evidence was heard that among the items found on board was a cooked fish that had been half eaten. Later on in the investigation, the fish was to prove a vital piece of evidence. It emerged the fish had been thrown to the *Brime* crew by a Clare fisherman the day before. He had been fishing in Irish waters, proving that the crew of the *Brime* were also within the Irish jurisdiction as they were within the 19-km limit covered by the Irish authorities. Fishermen from North Kerry had also seen the vessel within Irish waters.

On 22 March Judge O'Higgins told the jury that the importation charges had been withdrawn in the case. Van Onzen and Loopmans were both cross-examined before the evidence came to a close. According to the *Cork Examiner's* coverage of the trial, Van Onzen denied ordering the scuttling of the vessel and said such a move would have been suicide. Referring to his fears that the boarding party were the Mafia, he said: 'I could expect anything with two tonnes of hash on board.'

In his evidence, Loopmans said he was an experienced sailor, who had competed in yacht racing. He said he had been running a wine importation business with a silent partner, but this failed when the partner ran away with their finances for the business. He told the court that he had been approached and asked to sail a yacht. He was introduced to the rest of the *Brime* crew and they set off from Tenerife to collect the cannabis haul off the coast of Morocco. The crew were then ordered to sail with the cargo towards Ireland, where they were to drop anchor 80km west of Skellig Michael, off the coast of Kerry. The court heard that the *Brime* arrived at its destination on 8 or 9 July and waited to meet with a fishing boat to collect the cargo. Echoing Van Onzen, he said the crew had not intended to enter Irish waters, but had to change their plan when there was no contact from the vessel they were supposed to meet. They sailed northwards in the direction of Loop Head, hoping to meet the other boat and had decided to make contact by mobile phone, only as a last resort. The intended destination of the cargo was Wales. He said that he and Van Onzen both wanted to drop the cannabis into the sea when they saw an aircraft circle above them several times. He said Bland refused because he was in charge of the cargo.

Late the following day, guilty verdicts were returned by the jury on two charges each. They were found guilty of unlawful possession of cannabis resin within Irish territorial waters with intent to supply to another, and to being in possession of the drug, on 13 July. It had taken more than three-and-a-half hours to return the verdict. By then, the trial had gone on for three weeks. In recognition of the financial difficulties placed on the jury, as a result of the trial's length, Judge O'Higgins said he would write to the Minister for Justice to relate some of the jurors' views about the issue of personal recompense for what they had lost. He advised the concerned jurors to contact their local political representatives about their frustration with the existing system, which saw no payment for members of jury panels. The judge said it seemed unfortunate and unfair that people providing such a vitally important service should have to suffer loss and said there ought to be compensation for jurors who were self-employed.

The men were remanded in custody overnight for sentencing the following morning. Before they were sentenced, Inspector Jim Fitzgerald outlined the men's backgrounds to the judge. He said Van Onzen was born in 1957 and was one of eleven children. He said he and the other *Brime* crew members were offered stg£50,000 to carry out the job and that he had no previous convictions. Loopmans was born in 1963 and had three brothers and a sister. His sister had died at the age of eleven in an accident, which affected Loopmans deeply. His father had a number of business interests that went bust. The court was told he had a conviction for armed robbery in 1987, for which he had been given a three-year sentence. A letter written by his mother was read in court by his Senior Counsel, Séamus Sorahan, in which she said her son had received a good Catholic education.

In handing down his sentences, Judge O'Higgins singled out Sergeant Christopher McCarthy for the courage he had shown during the detention of the *Brime* and its crew. He asked that his comments be passed on to the then Garda Commissioner, Pat Culligan. Turning to the matter on hand, he said that Van Onzen and Loopmans were very seriously involved in the *Brime* operation but recognised that there were obviously bigger fish elsewhere who were connected to the crime.

Each were handed ten-year sentences for the charge of possession with intent to supply in Irish territorial waters. They were given seven-year sentences to run concurrently, for the charge of possession of the drug. They were to be backdated to when they were taken into custody on the previous 13 July. Judge O'Higgins also ordered the destruction of the drugs and the forfeiture of the boat by the State.

With the trial over, it was now time to focus on Fitzgerald and Bland. They had been watching the outcome of the trial with much interest, wondering how their guilty pleas would reflect on their own sentencing hearing. Judge O'Higgins presided over the hearing on 30 May. Both men also received ten-year sentences, but the judge made a distinction between them and their fellow crew mates because of their decision to plead guilty. As a result, Fitzgerald had two years suspended while Bland was given a three-year suspension.

Before the sentencing, the court heard that Fitzgerald was the youngest of six children. He had worked in the Sherriff Street An Post sorting office until 1988, when he resigned and went to Amsterdam. Bland was born in Boston but was raised in Lancashire in England and had a British passport. Inspector Fitzgerald said Bland was co-operative from the outset and Fitzgerald later admitted his involvement and co-operated with the investigation. The court heard that Bland had quelled the fears of the boarding party by telling them there were no explosives on board the ketch. In cross examination by Anthony Kennedy SC, Inspector Fitzgerald said that Bland was a bit of a loner, who had been hoping to get a better life as a result of the *Brime* operation. He had claimed he had been threatened while in custody and was moved to a separate wing of the prison he was in. He also told Gardaí he was worried that he was a marked man because of the money people behind the operation had lost as a result of the aborted drugs run. He had been a mechanic on the boat. Mr Kennedy said his client had been living in squalid conditions and fell to the temptation offered by the organisers of the *Brime* operation. He said Fitzgerald had also brought disaster on his life by getting involved. Judge O'Higgins recommended they serve their sentences in Mountjoy Prison, in Dublin.

With the sentencing over, appeals were lodged with the Courts Service. On 22 December 1994 Bland's sentence was reduced to five years in prison by the Court of Criminal Appeal. The three-judge court accepted he was suffering in prison. Mr Justice O'Flaherty said the court took the view that the sentence was excessive, particularly with regard to his co-operation with Gardaí. It was also accepted that he could not receive visits from close relatives, because he was in a foreign country. Appeals against their conviction by Van Onzen and Loopmans failed in December 1995. All four have since been released.

Judge O'Higgins's assertion in court that the crew members were not the main players in the operation was a reminder to the investigators that the mastermind of the operation was still at large. Following the seizure from the *Brime*, the focus returned quickly to David Huck. He had been living in Clare since the 1980s and owned substantial property in the county. He had tried to set up a wheelchair manufacturing business, but the venture did not get off the ground. Locals in Clare were unaware of the suspicions that hung over David in the UK. However, it emerged that he owned the *Brime* and attempts were made by the Gardaí to trace him. He had fled the country, not long after his release from custody in Cahersiveen, and could not be located.

Officers almost gave up hope of ever tracking him down. However, the British authorities struck gold when they captured him off the coast of England in October 1996. He and three others were arrested close to Cornwall, sailing a British-registered vessel called *Fata Morgana*. Customs seized 4 tonnes of cannabis in the operation, but heavy swells caused their vessel to sink and they lost the cannabis to the choppy seas. The operation, codenamed 'Jaegar', continued however, and a further thirteen people were arrested on-shore as part of it. The operation had been underway for almost a year and involved the co-operation of the Customs National Investigation Agency, the British Navy and the South West Regional Crime Squad in the UK.

There were fears that the loss of the cannabis could hamper

the prosecution's case. However, the concerns were unfounded. Huck was convicted of conspiring to smuggle cannabis resin into the UK, between November 1995 and October 1996, after a two-month trial at Exeter Crown Court in 1997. He was sentenced to fourteen years in prison. Judge Sean Overend said he had no doubt that Huck was a major player in the aborted drug smuggling exercise. According to the *Irish Independent*, the judge added: 'Without your knowledge of the sea and of smuggling and your ability to sail yachts across the oceans, none of this would have been possible.' During a previous court hearing, he referred to Huck as a buccaneer.

Huck has so far not been questioned about the *Brime* by Gardaí. However, the Criminal Assets Bureau (CAB) set the wheels in motion to seize his property in Aughinish, in Clare. The portfolio included a house and 4 hectares of land. The bureau secured a High Court injunction preventing Huck from reducing his assets in Ireland below £475,000 and was granted a tax judgement against him for more than £500,000. The only way to recoup the taxes from him was through the sale of his property. In May 2002 the CAB had a stroke of luck when a 1.6-hectare site, owned by Huck, overlooking Lough Derg in Clare, was sold off for €150,000. At an earlier auction, the highest bid for the property was €80,000 but the CAB had hoped to get €95,000 from the property. As a result, the property was not sold at auction, but later attracted the bigger sum in a bidding war between interested parties.

As the attention was focused on Huck and his property portfolio, efforts were being made by the Irish State to sell off the *Brime* – for the benefit of the Exchequer. The Department of Defence placed adverts in the media offering a ketch for sale, on 2 August 1996. No reference was made to the vessel's colourful background, but its anonymity was ended when a controversy erupted about whether the Department of Defence had the power to sell it. There was doubt over whether the trial judge had intended the vessel to go to the Department or the navy, when he made his forfeiture order. The saga continued right into 1998, when the vessel was eventually put up for sale again, along with four other vessels that the State had acquired.

In October of that year the then Minister for Defence, Michael Smith, addressed the issue in the Dáil. He said: 'Consideration was given to the question of refurbishing the vessel for use by the Naval Service. When it was taken over it was found to have a number of major defects and an expert survey was commissioned by the Department to ascertain the likely nature and cost of repairs. The findings indicated that extensive repairs would be necessary to bring the vessel up to naval service requirements at a cost which was considered to be uneconomic. Accordingly, a decision was taken on 1 October

1997, by the then Minister for Defence, to dispose of the vessel. Because of the need to clarify a number of legal issues in regard to ownership of the vessel it was not possible to finalise the sale arrangements before now.'

The sale of the vessel was eventually secured in 1998 when it was purchased for use in West Cork as a skipper charter vessel. The ketch was refurbished and renamed its original name, the *Xenios*.

Two years after the *Brime* capture, two officers involved in the operation were honoured by the Department of Defence. The department presented Lieutenant Commander Mellet and coxswain of the rib, Paddy Kennedy with Distinguished Service Medals.

KARMA

The radio played in the background as Michael Flynn slowly woke up. He was not paying much attention to what was being aired as the familiar sound of the news broadcast's jingle came out over the airwaves. However, when the newsreader mentioned that a yacht was being towed into Courtmachserry, the customs officer's ears pricked up. When the name of the troubled vessel was mentioned, something niggled at his brain.

He knew he had heard of a vessel in recent times with a similar name. He was not sure if it was the same one but he was not going to take a chance. Customs, Gardaí and the navy in Ireland had been warned to be on the lookout for a vessel called *Karma of the East* in recent weeks, as there were suspicions that it was involved in an international drug smuggling mission. If that were the case, it appeared that it could be in trouble off the coast of West Cork, possibly with a consignment of drugs on board. The officer decided to contact his colleague, Antóin MacMathúna, and travel with him to the picturesque harbour village. Michael picked him up in Cork city and they hurried westwards to Courtmacsherry – to make sure they would not be too late to check the vessel.

When the two men arrived, the pier was their first stop. A large crowd had gathered to see the arrival of the *Karma* into the safe harbour. The troubled vessel had only just reached the pier and its crew were in a relaxed mood. It was now around 11.00am, two hours after the news broadcast had been relayed over the national airwaves and alerted Michael Flynn. The yacht's crew members were hungry and tired, but they were also relieved that they were now safely on dry land. They had been travelling for weeks and were at the end of their tether because of problems with the engine, rudder and bilge of the yacht. However, none of them were prepared for a fire which broke out on board that morning, out to sea off the West Cork coast. The crew managed to extinguish the fire, but the engines then failed. As a result, the *Karma* began to drift aimlessly at sea, battling against high winds. At this point the crew knew it was time to call in the assistance of the lifeboat service.

The call for help was received in Courtmacsherry from the radio control base on Valentia Island at 7.36am on 23 July 1991. A crew of eight lifeboat volunteers travelled out to sea and met up with the stricken yacht. The four Cork men on board, including antiques dealer Christopher O'Connell, were ecstatic. The difficulties of recent days were coming to an end and they were nearly home. When they drew into the West Cork harbour, just after 11.00am, all they wanted was a good rest and fresh food.

However, their difficulties were far from over. Michael Flynn and Antóin MacMathúna were waiting for the crew and wanted to know where they were coming from. The four men told the officers that they had sailed the yacht from Galway and that they were delivering the boat to either Kinsale or Crosshaven for an Englishman. The crew said they had spent ten days in the Galway and Kinvara areas before travelling towards Cork. Although they knew MacMathúna and Flynn were customs officers, they did not appear excited or perturbed by their presence. Instead, they had many tales to relate of their time up the west coast of Ireland. However, the customs officers were sceptical. The weather had been bad in Ireland that summer, with very little sunshine. Despite this, the men all had tans, prompting the officers to wonder how this was the case, if they had only been as far as Galway on their travels. Also, the officers knew that the *Karma of the East* had been in Dartmouth in recent weeks.

The information had come to light through an English policeman, who made enquiries when he heard men speaking with Cork accents in Dartmouth. He was a regular visitor to Cork and recognised the accents immediately. He wondered why the men were in the area. When he made enquiries, he discovered a vessel called the *Karma of the East* had been chartered by a Corkman called Christopher O'Connell, and he decided to pass on the information to friends he had made in Cork, who happened to be Gardaí. His friends recognised the name of the man, mainly because he was an antiques dealer and gaming hall operator in the city centre. He was known locally as Golly O'Connell because of his hairstyle when he was younger. He had inherited the family business on Lavitt's Quay, which had previously been owned by his father and grandfather. However, it had come to the attention of Gardaí recently that he regularly associated with people involved in the drugs trade. These associations had not initially aroused too much suspicion, as he had friends and contacts in all sectors of society. However, when it emerged he had chartered a boat in the UK, local Gardaí began to question why the antiques dealer needed the yacht, and wondered if he had now become involved in the drugs trade.

The movements of the vessel were kept under surveillance, and it was known that it had gone close to the coast of Morocco. When the two officers arrived in Courtmacsherry and saw the boat that morning, they knew Michael Flynn's hunch was likely to be confirmed. They spoke with the crew and then decided it was time to get assistance from other colleagues. As it was before the advent of mobile phones, one of the men had to go to the local phone box and called the customs service in Cork for back up. They also alerted Gardaí in nearby Bandon.

The two customs officers decided to carry out a preliminary inspection of the yacht, while they waited for assistance. At this point, their suspicions were proven right. On board were large packages, wrapped in Hessian cloth with rope handles on either side. Christopher O'Connell said the packages were ballast to stabilise the boat. However, experience stood to the men and they knew that the wrapped packages held cannabis resin. By now, Gardaí had arrived and they arrested the four crew members, who were horrified that making a call for help had resulted in the sudden interest in their activities from the Irish law enforcement agencies. The tourist season had not yet kicked off in the village and the interests of the locals were also aroused by the mysterious cargo on board the yacht.

As the four men were taken to Bandon Garda station for questioning, a back-up team of customs officers arrived in the seaside village. A more intensive search was carried out and just under 700kg of cannabis was found on the yacht. The twenty-eight bales were hidden under floorboards beneath a bunk, in wardrobes and under seating on the boat. The quantity was enough to make up to seven million cannabis cigarettes and was worth almost £7 million. The bales had been loaded onto the vessel off Punta Nador, on the coast of

Morocco, on 16 July. Despite the intelligence received about the *Karma*, it is likely its arrival into Courtmacsherry would have gone unnoticed if Michael Flynn had not been listening to his radio. Customs officers and Gardaí working on the case were relieved that his vigilance had paid off. It was believed the haul was destined for Cork-based associates of a Dublin drugs gang, whose profits would now be hit because of Flynn's actions. The officers spent three days in Courtmacsherry, while locals flocked to the pier to see the activities around the hapless boat. When the intricate search was finished, the yacht was taken to Crosshaven for storage – while a case was pursued against the crew.

With the drugs to back up the case, a decision was taken to charge all four men in connection with the haul on the evening of their arrival. They were all charged with being in unlawful possession of cannabis resin and having a controlled drug in their possession for the purpose of sale or supply to persons unknown. One of the crew was the only one granted bail, and he was released on bonds totalling £55,000, while the other three were remanded in custody.

Remand hearings were held over the next number of months while the State's case against the four men was prepared. However, the prosecution of two of the men was dropped when Malachy Boohig, State solicitor for West Cork, made an application for the action at a sitting of Bandon

District Court on 31 October. Judge Brendan Wallace granted the application. Now, only the skipper and Christopher O'Connell remained to be dealt with through the justice system. Both men were now on bail, with Christopher O'Connell having been granted bail three days after he was originally charged. At the same hearing on 31 October, charges of intent to sell or supply cannabis resin were also withdrawn against both men. However, new charges of cannabis importation and conspiracy to import the drug were added to their indictments. The conspiracy charge related to dates before 2 May 1991, within the State, and dates between 2 May 1991 and 24 July 1991, outside the State's jurisdiction.

The men were then expecting to be sent forward for trial on all three charges, but an unexpected turn came when Judge Wallace discharged the importation charges during another sitting of Bandon District Court. A technical error had resulted in the charges referring to the 1979 Misuse of Drugs Act regulations instead of the 1988 regulations. As a result, the men and their defence teams were preparing to battle just one charge each when their cases came before the circuit court. Applications were made by both men to have the cases heard in Dublin, despite the seizure being made in Courtmacsherry and subsequent district court sittings also taking place in West Cork. The applications were granted under the Courts Act 1981 and the trial was scheduled to get underway in Dublin on 18 December 1992.

With the other two men released of all charges, Christopher O'Connell and the skipper were both hoping that the trial would go their way. However, their arraignment on 18 December did not go as smoothly as they expected. A further four charges each had been added to the men's indictments. When sending the men forward for trial on the single charge, Judge Wallace had indicated that the DPP could add further charges if he saw fit. Now, as well as the possession of cannabis charge, both men were also charged with possession of cannabis resin for sale or supply; importation of the drug; conspiracy to import cannabis resin; and importation of the controlled drug for sale or supply.

The men and their legal teams were shocked and a legal challenge was mounted to prevent the new charges being added to the indictments. Leave to apply for a judicial review was granted and the challenge was heard on 30 July 1993. In a reserved judgement, Mr Justice Ronan Keane dismissed the charges of importation and conspiracy to import. He declared that their addition to the indictments of Christopher O'Connell and the skipper was outside the powers of the DPP.

At this point, neither side was satisfied. The DPP took a case to the Supreme Court to argue that the addition of the importation and importation for sale or supply charges was within his remit. The higher court ruled that adding the new charges was not outside the powers of the DPP. However, an objection by O'Connell to the charge of importation for sale or supply was not allowed by the Supreme Court. The ruling from the three-judge court was delivered by Mrs Justice Susan Denham on 24 March 1994.

After such a protracted legal battle, the cases against both men were eventually scheduled to take place in Dublin Circuit Criminal Court in April 1995. However, another obstacle was put in the way one night, just days ahead of the trial. O'Connell and his wife had just pulled into the grounds of a restaurant on the Naas Road, in Dublin, when a group of men approached O'Connell, seconds after he got out of his car. One of the men shot him in the leg, and the three managed to escape from the scene without being caught. The injured man was rushed to hospital and the trial had to be postponed until the following October. Speculation abounded that those behind the shooting were trying to warn the antiques dealer not to reveal details about the drug smuggling operation during the trial.

The trial eventually got underway on 8 October 1995, before Judge Gerard Buchanan. Now, the men faced just three charges, as the charges of possession for sale or supply and conspiracy to import were no longer on the indictment. A crewmate of the *Karma of the East*, was one of the principal witnesses. Charges against him had been dropped in the early days of the investigation and the State felt he could be a vital cog in the prosecution wheel against the two accused men. He related how the wrapped bales had been loaded onto the yacht from another vessel at sea, and that Christopher O'Connell had told his fellow crew mates that the cargo was for him. He said they contained gold coins and antiques, an explanation that could be believed because of his background in the antiques trade.

One crew member was enlisted in the operation when he met Christopher O'Connell and the skipper in Kinsale on 9 June 1991 – more than a month before the arrival of the stricken vessel into West Cork. He had a background in sailing and was desperate for work. He already knew the skipper and asked him if he knew of any work available, and was told there could be work within a few weeks. He was contacted shortly afterwards and was told that there was a job involving the collection of Americans in the Algarve to take them on a coastal cruise of Spain and Portugal. He told the skipper he was interested and flew to England to pick up the *Karma* in Dartmouth with a group of four other men, including the skipper and Christopher O'Connell. Christopher O'Connell left the group to fly home because of a family matter. However, the Cork men and the two other men made their way towards the Algarve to collect the Americans. One of the group was later forced to fly home after becoming ill. In the early stages of the voyage, the men were accompanied by an Englishman and his partner.

The Englishman was the owner of the *Karma of the East*. He bought it in the late 1980s when he had an ambition to sail around the world. Two years later, he decided to charter it and contacted agents to get clients for the vessel. As a result, he was approached by Christopher O'Connell and the skipper in May 1991. The charter was for a six-week period, at a cost of £6,000. The owner told the trial that it was intimated at the meeting that the Cork man would be the skipper for the duration of the charter. At the skipper's request, the owner agreed to install a global positioning system. A deposit of £1,500 in cash was handed over by Christopher O'Connell. He paid the remainder of the fee in June. When the *Karma* left Dartmouth, the owner and his partner decided to travel with the crew as far as the French port of Brest. It was obvious, even at this early stage, that the yacht was going to cause the crew problems. In the English Channel, his expertise had to be called on when the yacht experienced engine trouble. Further repairs were carried out when the vessel pulled into the Breton port of Cameret.

The problems continued after the owner and his partner left the yacht in Brest. The crew were later forced to stop off at a port in Galicia, in northern Spain, with further problems. At this point, the skipper called the owner of the boat for advice about the autopilot. The yacht owner later explained that work was being carried out to prepare the yacht for the journey, when O'Connell and his crew members arrived in Dartmouth ahead of schedule.

After these problems, the owner heard no more from the group. They continued their journey southwards, stopping off at Oporto, where they were met by Christopher O'Connell and a friend of his. The group then arrived into Villamoro on the Algarve, where they were scheduled to pick up the Americans for their cruise. Christopher O'Connell had met the American at a greyhound race meeting and became friendly with him. According to O'Connell, the American had paid the expenses for chartering the boat before Christopher O'Connell paid the owner. The couple did not go on the cruise but did meet with Christopher O'Connell. When Christopher O'Connell returned to the boat, he told his fellow crew that they would travel further south towards Morocco to collect coins and artefacts for a contact he had met through his American acquaintance. One crew member told the court that the crew remained offshore from Morocco and that another vessel eventually pulled up alongside them. Radio contact had been made to the *Karma* crew before the arrival of the other vessel. Two French-speaking men on board the other boat loaded bales onto the *Karma of the East* before rapidly leaving the scene. The boat then began the journey home towards Cork, experiencing further difficulties before the alarm was raised near Courtmacsherry. By that point, the vessel had travelled more than 3,862km from Dartmouth to close to Morocco and back towards Ireland.

The trial was receiving daily coverage in the media, satisfying the public's fascination with the chance seizure of the cannabis resin. However, the coverage resulted in the abortion of the trial after four days – because newspaper reports had referred to the amount of cannabis that was found on the ship. The coverage was deemed prejudicial – because the amount had not been revealed to the jury in the trial at that point. The jury was discharged and a new date for the trial was set for 22 April 1996. The two accused men were remanded on continuing bail, until the new trial got underway under Judge Dominic Lynch.

Giving evidence in the new trial, Michael Flynn outlined to the court what he and his colleague had seen when they arrived in Courtmacsherry. He said Christopher O'Connell and another crew member had come off the boat at that point but the customs officers ordered them back on it. During a preliminary search, MacMathúna found the bales when he looked under the floorboards.

It emerged that the skipper had been promised between £12,000 and £15,000 to take part in the venture. However, he told Gardaí that he had been hired initially by his co-accused to be the skipper of the *Karma* on a coastal cruise for the American man. The fee promised for that job was £12,000. He refused the offer, at first, but took it up when Christopher O'Connell contacted him a second time about it. This was later upgraded in Villamoro when Christopher O'Connell asked him to take the boat on a 'treasure hunt' for gold coins. Sergeant Mary Dalton said the skipper outlined to Gardaí that he had known Christopher O'Connell already but that the pair had not met for twenty years. Christopher O'Connell made contact with him in February 1991, six months before the *Karma* limped into Courtmacsherry, to ask him to become involved in the sailing mission. The skipper had been an obvious choice – he was well known as a sailor and regularly competed in races, until he retired from the sport in 1982. He had sailed in seven of the Fastnet races and had been selected by Christopher O'Connell because of his experience in sailing.

In his statement to Gardaí, the skipper denied knowing that the bales contained drugs instead of gold coins. He said he would have 'been cuckoo to leave that stuff on board' if he had known the bales contained cannabis. He estimated to Gardaí that the operation must have cost £1 million to mount and that his co-accused was only a small cog in the overall operation. He explained: 'He wouldn't have that kind of money'.

Speaking in court, the skipper said the *Karma of the Ea*st arrived at Villamoro to pick up the American. Christopher O'Connell got off the vessel to meet with the couple, whom he already knew. He was off the boat for a considerable amount of time, but came back on one occasion to borrow a chart. When he brought it back, a location point off the Moroccan coast had been marked in on it. He told his fellow crew that the clients had changed their minds and that he now had a new job. He had met an Irish-American diver through the couple and he had asked Christopher O'Connell to travel towards Morocco to pick up artefacts and gold coins for him. Christopher O'Connell asked the skipper if he would mind and the skipper agreed to the request, suspecting nothing unusual. The point marked on the chart was the location where the materials were to be picked up. The *Karma of the East* continued its journey southwards towards that point. He said the destination of the yacht was either Crosshaven or Kinsale.

Investigators believed that Christopher O'Connell had expected someone to meet the *Karma* at sea to offload the cargo. As the vessel approached the Irish coast, the antiques dealer regularly looked out to sea with binoculars. He claimed in evidence to the court that he was duped into importing the cannabis by the diver, who had asked him to collect the 'artefacts and gold coins' off Morocco. He said the diver claimed to have known Kinsale well and that he had worked for a man who took in valuable gold and bronze items from the wreck of the *Lusitania* ship, off the Old Head of Kinsale, and from other wrecks off the Irish coast. According to Christopher O'Connell, the diver said he had shipped a lot of these items for this man to England. However, a detective who had worked on the case, James O'Riordan, told the court that the man's widow said her husband had never been involved in taking materials from the *Lusitania*, which had been torpedoed off the Irish coast in 1915 during World War I.

According to Christopher O'Connell, his link to the seizure of the cannabis resin was not his fault. He said: 'I was either set up by my friend or by [the diver] or both.' He claimed the diver asked him to bring back some parcels of coins and other artefacts to Ireland. He agreed he had collected the *Karma* for the American to cruise on. When he met them by appointment at Villamoro, there was friction between them and they had decided against the cruise. This was when the diver came up with the alternative job for the crew of the *Karma*. The American introduced the diver, as a friend of his, to Christopher O'Connell. Christopher O'Connell said: 'I thought it would be a nice gesture to help out a friend of the man who paid for the hire of the yacht and I agreed.' He said it didn't ever cross his mind he would be given bales of cannabis to bring back to Ireland. He added: 'There is nobody in this court more anti-drugs than me.'

His defence, however, was not accepted by the jury. After more than three hours, they returned to the courtroom with a ten to two majority, at the end of the five-day trial.Christopher O'Connell was convicted of importation of cannabis resin, importation of cannabis resin for sale or supply and possession of cannabis resin. The skipper was acquitted. The verdict was returned on Friday, 26 April 1996 – more than five years after the crime itself. The sentencing was adjourned to the following Monday. At the hearing, Judge Lynch handed down two concurrent eight-year sentences and one four-year sentence. All three were to run concurrently, from 27 April 1996. He refused leave to appeal the conviction and sentence.

With the investigation over, it was now accepted that the *Karma of the East* had not been owned by anyone involved in the importation attempt. The vessel had been seized by the Irish authorities to allow the search and investigation. However, the vessel was then returned to its owner, who had no role to play in the botched importation.

As he and the crew members of the *Karma of the East* were getting their lives back on track, Christopher O'Connell began his jail sentence. Although no further attempt had been made to threaten Christopher O'Connell's life, the memory of what had happened prior to the original trial date still hung over him. He was under armed protection throughout the trial, a fact that was hidden from the jury. However, he himself did refer to the incident at the restaurant on the Naas Road, during his evidence, when he said: 'I ended up getting shot about a year ago. I was getting too close.' During his sentencing hearing, his defence counsel Barry White told the court that his client might have to serve his sentence in solitary confinement because of concerns for his safety.

Christopher O'Connell's time in prison gained a lot of media attention, when he was moved from Wheatfield prison to the open prison in Shelton Abbey, near Arklow, just months after he was sentenced. The Wicklow low-security prison is generally used as a unit where long-term offenders can prepare for release as they come close to the end of their sentence. It holds fifty-six prisoners. The movement of Christopher O'Connell to the prison raised the hackles of Fianna Fáil's Justice spokesman John O'Donoghue. He declared: 'We have got to send out a clear message to people involved in drugs and crime that they had better think again – the laws and procedures in this country are too lax and need to be changed.' The controversial prisoner was returned to Mountjoy later that year.

Christopher O'Connell has since been released from prison and is rarely seen in his native Cork. His life as a well-known businessman in the city was brought to an end by the call of distress made from the *Karma of the East*.

Chapter 7

URLINGFORD

Seán was nervous as he picked up the phone to make one of the riskiest calls of his entire life. He hoped his powers of persuasion were good. His safety – and his family's – depended on how convincing he sounded. Seán knew, as well, that taking on the job he was being offered would put immense pressure on him to deliver. The Irish authorities were relying on him to help them get, what they hoped, would be a major coup in stemming the flow of drugs into Ireland. It had taken weeks to get this far in the operation.

Putting his concerns aside, Seán dialled the number and waited for the call to ring out. A man with a foreign accent answered and Seán warily introduced himself to the stranger. It was a surreal feeling, posing as a drugs trafficker. It was strange also knowing that the man he had called was speaking to him from a ship carrying huge quantities of an illegal drug, some of which were bound for ready markets in Ireland and other parts of Europe. It was weird too, to be making arrangements to collect the portion destined for Ireland, because his usual role was helping in the confiscation of such cargoes.

This time, things were different. Seán was a navy officer, who had been enlisted in a top secret operation. His role now was to act as an undercover contact. He was entrusted with contacting the traffickers and arranging to meet at sea to transfer the precious cargo of cannabis resin and return with it to Ireland. It was hoped the bold move would help smash a key drug smuggling operation in Dublin. Although it was risky, Seán liked the challenge and accepted the offer. A colleague stayed on shore to control naval operations and to keep communication channels open, via satellite, between Seán and the naval vessel carrying out the surveillance. The shore-based naval officer had the benefit of Maritime Patrol Aircraft information on traffic in the area. He also ensured that military superiors and his Garda liaison officer were being kept informed during the operation.

It was October 1995 in Dublin when the Gardaí approached the navy with crucial information. A major shipment of cannabis resin was heading north towards Ireland's coast. Gardaí had learned that it was planned to transfer huge amounts of the illegal substance to another vessel, which was scheduled to sail into one of the hundreds of quiet, sheltered inlets off the south coast with its cargo. The haul would then be distributed to Dublin criminals, who were anxiously awaiting its arrival. Gardaí aimed to infiltrate the organisation and control the delivery of the drugs into Ireland. Plans were drawn up for the undercover project, which was to take place just two months ahead of the formal establishment of the Garda National Drugs Unit on 1 January 1996. Some senior figures had already been appointed to the new unit and were directing the undercover operation. As part of the project, a major surveillance operation had taken place and meetings were held by officers in Dublin and Cork to ensure all would go according to plan. With the promised support of the navy, all was ready for the initiative.

However, the Irish agencies were not acting alone. On the other side of the Atlantic, efforts were underway by the United States Drug Enforcement Agency (DEA) to stifle the successes of a major drug trafficking network that had links all over the world. Working closely with law enforcement agencies in the US, Canada and Europe, the agency knew that Irish authorities could also help in the operation. Up to this point, close liaisons between the Irish law enforcement agencies and their international counterparts had not been clearly evident and Gardaí were hoping that the international operation they had become involved in would help to strengthen bonds.

They placed surveillance on senior individuals in the Dublin drug trade in October 1995. Information derived from the operation revealed the targets were hatching a major importation operation. A meeting in Cork had sparked considerable interest among Gardaí. Their target had been seen with an American-based visitor, who officers knew, from their US counterparts, to be involved in the international drugs trade. Other American-based drug trafficking suspects had also visited Ireland in recent times. For Gardaí the message was clear – it was time to act.

Just prior to this, a joint national drugs taskforce had been set up involving the Gardaí, the navy and the customs service in a bid to ease divisions between the enforcement agencies charged with drug interdiction. Armed with their information and knowing they had a contact on board the vessel heading towards Ireland, Gardaí approached the navy looking for help with their operation. Key to the plan would be the success in duping those aboard the mother ship planning to rendezvous at sea with Irish criminals. This was where Seán came into the frame. Gardaí had given him the phone number for the contact on board the mother ship. The rest was up to him.

Now, as he made his initial contact with the man on board the vessel, he managed to persuade the foreigner that all was well on the Irish side, and urge him eventually to move the mother ship, the *Master Star*, further north towards Ireland. As far as the man on board the ship believed, the 'gang' Seán was representing had put the necessary measures in place to ensure a vessel would meet the *Master Star* – also called the *Tropic Moon* – at sea to collect the cannabis designated for them. The Irish share of 13.5 tonnes was just a tiny percentage of the overall load on board. A total of 400 tonnes of the valuable substance was to be dropped off to a flotilla of smaller vessels as the mother ship travelled westwards towards the Americas, after dropping the Irish consignment.

Seán made a number of phone calls to his contact on board the *Master Star*, while moves were underway on mainland Ireland to prepare for the sea transfer. A vessel was needed to sail out to meet the bigger ship, and a fisherman was approached in West Cork to help in this aspect of the operation. A fishing trawler was thought to be the best option for the job, because it would have a big derrick for moving the cargo on board. The fisherman had been concerned about becoming involved in such a risky operation but officers managed to ease his fears. Selecting a crew to travel on board the trawler was the next step. Being selected for the undercover operation was a coup for each individual. However, each of them also knew they were taking on a job which held a major element of danger – if the crew on board the *Master Star* realised they were being set up.

The Irish authorities were well aware of the risks involved and arranged a naval vessel to travel to sea, close to the trawler. An air craft was also enlisted to travel overhead, to help in locating the mother ship. Intense efforts were put in by naval officers to trace the ship, with the use of radar and other tracking equipment, as it arrived into the Bay of Biscay.

Hopes were high when the team of Gardaí, accompanied by Seán and the trawler owner, left the fishing port of Castletownbere on 25 October. The trawler travelled for a few days to reach the location Seán had agreed with his contact and was shadowed by the crew of the *LE Aisling* naval vessel. However, despite their best efforts, the *Master Star* could not be located and severe weather conditions forced the team to abort the operation. The disappointed team headed back to Castletownbere without the planned cargo. However, it was not time to give up yet.

In early November, a second attempt was made and the team again left Castletownbere, this time under the surveillance of a naval crew on board the *LE Deirdre*. The trawler travelled for a few days before reaching the designated location, where the rendezvous was to take place. Once more, weather conditions were unfavourable and the trawler suffered some damage from the high waves. However, the crew persisted and this time, Seán's efforts in persuading his contact that he was *bone fide* paid off. Under the careful eye of the *LE Deirdre*, the two vessels finally met each other, in what was a game of high risk poker for the crew on the trawler.

The onus was on Seán to recognise the mother ship. He had been given details by his contact during their phone conversations from the safety of land. On spotting it at sea, he and his fellow crew members on the trawler weighed up the risk fac-tors, to ensure maximum safety, before making contact with the man by radio. Although the two men had been in contact with each other a number of times in recent weeks, they did not know what each other looked like and they never would. When Seán linked up with the man this time, they came to an arrangement to sail into quiet waters, away from the main shipping lanes, where they would have aroused the suspicion of other sea-going vessels.

The crew on board the small trawler marvelled at the sight of the mother ship and what was on it. They could see it was an ocean-going tug that had been greatly modified. There were up to twenty people on board, including women and children. As the operation got underway to transfer the Irish consignment onto the trawler, it became clear that the children were more than just guests – they were working on the *Master Star*. Under the supervision of adults on board, they were helping to unload the cannabis onto the trawler. They had no shoes and were not wearing any protective clothing. From what the Irish crew could see, those on board the mother ship appeared to be South American people, some with straps of cartridges of bullets worn across their torsos. One source described it afterwards as a float-ing supermarket of drugs. The vessel had come from the Azores but it was thought the consignment of cannabis had originated in Pakistan.

The operation on the *Master Star* was highly organised, with spare propellers and diving gear visible to the crew on board the Irish trawler. The tug was home to the crew for several weeks and evidence of domesticity could also be seen – a line of washed clothes flew in the breeze, and a number of dogs were on board.

The crew on the trawler had never seen anything like the *Master Star*, but they did not have much time to think about the strange sight before their eyes. Their efforts were instead put into receiving the 13.5 tonnes of cannabis from the tug. The crews of both vessels worked steadily over several hours, with the Irish team hoping their cover would not be blown. Eventually, the last bale was secured on board the trawler and the two vessels separated to head in different directions. As the *Master Star* continued its journey westwards, the trawler began the return journey to the south coast of Ireland. The first step of the undercover operation had been successful and the crew of the trawler felt nothing could go wrong now.

The original plan had been to bring the cargo into Schull, but a decision was then taken to bring it into the more private pier on Dinish Island, in the harbour of Castletownbere. In the dead of night, it was thought that nobody would notice the arrival of the trawler and the unloading of its precious cargo. If the venture was to be a success, it was vital that details of the operation did not leak out before the drug dealers, being targeted through the operation, were apprehended. A lorry had been brought from Dublin to take the cannabis resin away from Castletownbere, for collection by the criminals in the capital, who were expecting it. It took a couple of hours to complete the transfer from the trawler to the lorry. Gardaí were on duty in the area to prevent access to the pier. Some locals did notice the discreet Garda presence, and suspicions began to emerge about what exactly was happening.

The drugs were whisked away by the driver of the lorry, who was an undercover Garda officer. As he travelled towards Dublin, on the main road from Cork, he was unaware of the suspicions beginning to emerge in West Cork. On the southern side of Urlingford, he parked the 12m container which had been attached to the lorry and drove away from the scene. Members of the Gardaí awaited its arrival and put the container under surveillance, confident the Dublin criminals expecting the drugs would soon turn up to collect their wares. However, the grand plan was about to run in to massive difficulties.

By now, the rumour mill was rife and the media had been tipped off that something unusual was afoot in Castletownbere. When one journalist contacted a member of the navy about the presence of Gardaí in the West Cork fishing port, he knew the operation was in danger of being exposed, putting the team involved in the undercover mission at r   isk.

Meanwhile, near Urlingford, the Gardaí keeping the container under surveillance were also getting uneasy as their targets failed to turn up.

The targeted figures had become suspicious about the shipment and had opted not to travel to Urlingford. As well as that, four men were arrested in Finglas after Gardaí stopped a car carrying one of the main men they had been trying to ensnare with the elaborate undercover operation. One of those arrested was a man named John Noonan. Known as the Manager, he was from Fairways in Finglas, and was one of those seen meeting the American figure in Cork in mid-October. The four were questioned by Gardaí but were eventually released without charge. However, more than £230,000 had also been seized in the operation and was retained by Gardaí after the release of the four prisoners.

As details of the arrests began to emerge, the general public was enthralled by news that Ireland's largest ever consignment of cannabis had been seized by Gardaí in Urlingford. Knowing their prey were not going to turn up, officers had moved in and 'seized' the consignment in a blaze of publicity. The general public had no idea of the events that had led to the seizure or about the transfer at sea to the trawler crewed by Gardaí and the naval officer.

The huge haul was taken to Dublin for forensic analysis, under armed escort. An examination of the haul showed there was sand mixed in with the drug, prompting speculation that the cannabis could have come from either Morocco or Pakistan. A month after the seizure, the cannabis was transported to the ESB power plant in Rhode, in Offaly, to be destroyed, as part of routine practice. Some samples were retained from the haul, in the event of a court case involving any suspects behind the attempted importation.

In the immediate aftermath of the events in Urlingford, politicians, including Minister for Justice Nora Owen, showered praise on the law enforcement agencies . The following day in the Dáil, leader of the opposition, Bertie Ahern of Fianna Fáil, said: 'I congratulate the naval service, the Garda and the other arms of State involved in yesterday's activities although, unfortunately, it appears that the drug barons behind this haul have escaped once again. I wish the Garda well in apprehending them.' In response, the Taoiseach, Fine Gael's John Bruton, said: 'Obviously, one would not expect to find the drug barons in the lorry. That they were not apprehended on the spot should not warrant the significance Deputy Ahern attaches to it.' He added that congratulations should be extended to those involved in the seizure 'rather than trying to make much of the fact that the drug barons were not found in the cab of the lorry when it was found'.

However, the fact that the lorry driver was not arrested and questioned was set to dominate the fallout in the wake of the

Urlingford events. With no other arrests relating directly to the seizure, concern about the operation was beginning to mount. A major figure on the international drug smuggling scene was suspected of being the kingpin behind the operation. A file on the matter was prepared for the DPP for consideration. However, neither he nor the four arrested in Finglas were ever charged in connection with the seizure.

By the following spring, concern was rising that those behind the importation effort would escape the rigours of the law, just as the Dáil was preparing to debate the introduction of stronger drug trafficking legislation. The Drug Trafficking Bill proposed to extend the detention of suspected traffickers to seven days, with the permission of a Chief Superintendent. At the time, suspects could only be held for a period of twelve hours. During the Dáil debate on the bill, Bertie Ahern voiced his concerns about the Urlingford seizure: 'On 9 November, the day after the Urlingford drugs consignment find, I asked that the Drug Trafficking Bill be brought forward as I raised the fact that nobody had been apprehended at the location of the drugs find in Urlingford. Much has been written about that outside this House.'

Deputy Ahern was not alone in voicing his concerns. By now, there was speculation in the press that the Urlingford seizure was not as clear cut as it first seemed. The Dáil debate followed confidential briefings given to Fianna Fáil's John

O'Donoghue and the Progressive Democrats' Liz O'Donnell by Gardaí the previous weekend in their capacities as Justice spokespersons for their parties. The involvement of the law enforcement agencies in the operation leading to the Urlingford seizure was now becoming apparent, explaining why there had been no immediate arrests. Before the 6 March debate on the drug trafficking bill, Deputy O'Donnell challenged the Government's defence of the circumstances leading to the seizure. Quoted in the *Cork Examiner,* she suggested the legality of the operation was in question and wondered if the drugs had been imported into Irish territory with the knowledge of Government ministers. She added: 'I remain of the opinion that there are grounds to believe that the public was seriously misled over a prolonged period of time as to the nature of the operation, its motivation and its outcome.'

By now, there was speculation that money could have been paid over for the cannabis haul by Gardaí – in a bid to break up the gang being targeted in the undercover operation. However, this was rubbished by Minister Owen when speaking in the Dáil on the matter again on 7 March. She said: 'This is absolutely without foundation . . . The destruction of the drugs represented a very definite gain for the people of this country and, indeed, other countries, and a very definite loss for major criminals and not for the taxpayers.' Referring to the speculation about ministerial approval for the importation, she declared: 'On the question as to the level at which the importation was authorised, it was an operational decision and did not involve any politicians. The implementation of any Garda operation is a matter which is the responsibility of the relevant senior gardaí involved in any operation.'

As the controversy continued, Garda authorities felt it was now time to step in to clear up issues which had begun to overshadow the seizure itself. A strong statement was issued by the Garda Press Office on 10 March, claiming that lives were being put in danger by the on-going debate. The statement said: 'It is very disquieting to have publicly debated, on a daily basis, the intricacies of Garda operations, particularly when they have certain inaccuracies and have the potential for jeopardising on-going operations and the placing of some people in a life-threatening situation.' It also declared that all Garda operations and investigations were governed by procedures and legislative controls. It added: 'Such was the case in the Garda seizure of 13.5 tonnes of cannabis in November 1995, and the subsequent investigation. No breaches of procedure or legislation occurred. According to the statement, there were three negative results from the controversy – lives were being threatened, the international investigation had been seriously damaged, and the victims of drug-related crime became the losers, while the beneficiaries were those who made a living from crime.

However, the intervention by the Garda Press Office failed to quell the disquiet. A year on from the seizure, Minister Owen was again forced to refer to the matter. In a written answer to a Dáil question put down by Fianna Fáil's John O'Donoghue, she said: 'I am informed by the Garda Commissioner he is satisfied that there is nothing relating to this seizure which would suggest that a Garda investigation is required. He does not, therefore, intend to conduct an investigation into the matter.'

The Garda Commissioner, Pat Byrne, also felt it was time to hit back at the critics. He was critical of the portrayal of the operation in the media, particularly because the Urlingford seizure was regularly labelled as a sting. In contrast, the authorities referred to the incident as a 'controlled delivery' of the drugs in a bid to target the gang that the drugs were destined for. The *Cork Examiner* reported that at a meeting of the Association of European Journalists that same month, Commissioner Byrne said: 'The "sting" is used in other countries regularly but we cannot use it legally so we won't use it. It has been described as a sting operation which went wrong. From my experience a sting is where an agency provides its own bait to entrap culprits.'

Although Gardaí had expressed the fear that the international investigation had been hampered by the raging controversy in the Dáil and in the media, efforts continued both in Ireland and in the US to target the suspects behind the cannabis deal. The *Master Star* had continued on its journey northwestwards towards the US and Canada and was later detained by Canadian authorities as it floated into New-foundland. Since the events in Ireland in November 1995, Gardaí had kept in close contact with the London office of the DEA in relation to intelligence they had gathered on the movers behind the plot to import the cannabis into Ireland. The Gardaí also liaised directly with the DEA in the US, with some officers travelling to Washington to work with their US counterparts for a short period.

The co-operation paid off. DEA agents managed to infil-trate the US-based gang behind the foiled Irish importation. This led to the arrests in January 1997 of major movers in Los Angeles, after a consignment of drugs was coopered off the coast of Hawaii and taken into the US, through the Califor-nian coast in December 1996. The haul, totalling 17.5 tonnes of cannabis, had been off-loaded at sea onto a barge that was carrying undercover DEA agents from the Los Angeles field division. The drugs were then transported to Los Angeles, where agents made three deliveries of more than 4 tonnes each to Montreal, New York and the Los Angeles area. At that time, it was the largest quantity of hashish ever confiscated by US officials during an undercover operation.

Among those arrested, as a result of that sting, was an American-based New Zealander called Gary Matsuzaki, who had been in Ireland before the Urlingford events. He was arrested as part of an operation by law enforcement agencies targeting drug deliveries to Australia, Canada and the eastern United States. His key lieutenant, Brian Auchard, was also arrested and charged. Both were charged with the use of a communication device to facilitate the distribution of hashish. Matsuzaki was also convicted of being an accessory after the fact. He was sentenced to six years in prison and was released on 15 November 2002. Auchard was released on 18 July 2000, after a four-year sentence. So successful was the overall operation that former Los Angeles-based special agent Abel Reynoso said it was a case which could have been turned into a major movie.

Back in Ireland, John Noonan was still on the radar of Gardaí. He had fought to have the money seized in November 1995 returned to him, but it was eventually confiscated through a court order. He was not charged with any offence relating to it, but the heat was about to come down on him again. In February 1998 he was escorted back to Ireland, on a flight from Britain, to face a charge relating to the seizure of £27,000 of ecstasy tablets in Walkinstown the previous May. He had been charged in connection with the haul the previous year, but the charges were struck out in October because the Book of Evidence in the case was not ready. Warrants were later obtained by Gardaí for his re-arrest but by then he had moved abroad. He was traced to England and was arrested in Birmingham on 20 January 1998, in a joint operation between Gardaí and West Midlands police. A court in Birmingham ordered Noonan's extradition to face the new charge. On 21 July 1999 Noonan was jailed for eight years by Judge Kevin O'Connor after pleading guilty to possession of the ecstasy tablets at Greenhills Road, Walkinstown on 10 May 1997. He limped into court on crutches. In court, Det Garda Patricia McGarrity said it was rare to catch a drug dealer as significant as Noonan in possession of drugs. She said Gardaí believed he was a serious distributor and not the type to sell drugs on a street corner. She said 1,851 tablets had been found in the back of his car.

Nobody has ever been charged in connection with the Urlingford seizure. Although it was one of the most controversial chapters in the history of the Garda drug enforcement, sources in Ireland, and in the US, believe the overall achievement of the arrests of major figures in the US were greatly aided by information gained through the Irish undercover operation.

Note: Seán not real name.

Chapter 8

PLONGEUR WISKY

The cabin cruiser, *Plongeur Wisky*, had been travelling for more than a week when it reached Cappagh Pier in Kilrush on 1 November 1996. It had left Gibraltar on 23 October, with the intention of pulling into Donegal in late October. The boat's skipper, Kevin Lafferty from Malin Head, was frustrated as he had been hoping to arrive in his native county on schedule. However, engine trouble scuppered his plans and there was no option other than to pull into the Shannon estuary.

The arrival of the vessel came just three months after the arrival of the *Front Guider* into nearby Moneypoint – 50kg of cocaine was found on board that vessel. Another high profile operation followed, in September of that year, when 599kg of cocaine was found on board the *Sea Mist* in Cobh. As a result, the possibility of drug shipments being sneaked into Ireland, through the rugged coastline, was entrenched on people's minds, especially those living near the sea.

A man who saw the *Plongeur Wisky* arriving off the Clare

coast felt there was something unusual about the vessel. For a start, a craft like the cabin cruiser was a strange sight in winter, when the weather would not be suitable for pleasure activity. Secondly, the cruiser was circling around in the Shannon estuary, as the crew members on board tried to sort out the engine problems. He decided it was best to contact the customs service, which always welcomed information about any suspicious maritime activity. A Customs Drugs Watch programme was in place, through which coastal residents had been educated on how to identify suspect vessels in their area. The man, who saw the *Plongeur Wisky*, picked up the phone and made the call. After all, if the crew on board had nothing to hide, they would not mind being approached by customs. If, on the other hand, they were attempting to smuggle in drugs, they would be caught before they received the haul.

When customs received the call, officers based in the Tralee office were sent out to the Shannon estuary to check out the information received from the coastal contact. Winds had blown up and the sea was rough, when they reached the northern side of the Shannon estuary. When the officers arrived into Kilrush, they immediately saw the suspect vessel. Attempts to mend the engine problems had failed and the decision had been taken by the crew to pull into Kilrush harbour. Efforts to anchor were failing but the cabin cruiser eventually managed to dock in Cappagh pier. The customs officers decided to go onto the vessel – to determine if it was being used for any illegal activity. Lafferty and two other crew members, Andrew Kelly from Birmingham and Desmond McElroy from Ballymena, in Antrim, were on board and were being interviewed by the customs personnel. The officers called for back-up from their own drugs team and from the Gardaí.

While the men waited for their colleagues, they took a quick look around the vessel and found enough evidence to know that their contact's hunch was proven right. It was a Friday evening and hopes of a work-free weekend were dashed when suspect bales were found underneath the flooring of one of the cabins. Given that the bales had been hidden from view, the officers knew they had come upon an effort to smuggle contraband, of some description, on board the 14m *Plongeur Wisky*. When the back-up customs team and Gardaí arrived, Lafferty and his two crew mates were arrested and taken into custody. As they were being led away for questioning, decisions were being made on the most effective way to carry out an intricate search of the vessel. It was lifted onto dry land and moved to Kilrush Creek Marina, the following morning, to facilitate the search, which was to unearth a haul of 1.7 tonnes of cannabis resin. The bales each contained 25kg of the drug. A value of £16 million was put on the consignment.

Content with their seizure, officers knew the capture was due mainly to the engine difficulties experienced by the vessel, and the vigilance of their coastal contact. When news came through about events in Kilrush, Gardaí in Donegal became suspicious that five men arrested there two days before the *Plongeur Wisky* seizure had been connected to the vessel. Officers had arrested the men on Malin Head on 30 October, after they had stumbled on what they first believed were activities relating to paramilitaries. However, the men had been released just hours before suspicious arose cast over the arrival of the *Plongeur Wisky* into Kilrush.

Now that the drugs had been found on board the vessel and there was a known link to Malin, Gardaí believed there was a connection between the smuggling attempt and the arrests in Donegal. Adding to their suspicions was that the five in Donegal all had Antrim addresses, as had one of the men in custody in Clare. The Donegal five had been arrested after Gardaí became suspicious about them, when they met them near where an inflatable boat had bashed off rocks near Glengad, the evening before. Officers had been told by locals about the incident and had gone there to help recover the boat, as no suspicions had been aroused at that point. However, it became evident that all was not as it appeared, when officers met four men at the scene, who gave contradictory stories about how many people had been on the dinghy when it ran into trouble. At first, the men said there were only two, but this figure later rose to four before being brought back to two again.

After careful consideration, a decision was taken to arrest the men. A jeep was seized and examined by officers. Three of the arrested men had been standing near the jeep, when officers had first arrived at the scene. One of them said he owned the rib. The fourth man was down at the shore with the rib. A fifth man arrived at the scene, after Gardaí, and he was also arrested.

A search of the surrounding area resulted in the discovery of a radio scanner, camouflage netting, food and sleeping bags. It was clear that the men had intended being away from home for at least one night. The Gardaí were curious to know why the men needed a radio scanner. Drugs were the last things on the Gardaí's minds at this stage. Being so close to the border, officers believed the men were in the area for an IRA-related mission, particularly as their arrests came just days after an arms find in nearby Ballygorman. However, no arms were discovered in the latest operation on Malin Head.

They had been arrested under Section 30 of the Offences Against the State Act on suspicion of membership of the IRA. They were later released without charge.

A decision was taken to charge all three with the unlawful importation of cannabis resin. They were also charged with possession of the drug for sale or supply at Cappagh, Kilrush. The three men were brought before Judge Joseph Mangan, at a special weekend sitting of Kilrush District Court. They were granted free legal aid. The men were remanded in custody to Limerick Prison.

At the hearing, Sgt Noel Kinsella gave evidence of charging and cautioning thirty-two-year-old Lafferty from Bunn, Culkenny on Malin Head, on Saturday, 2 November at 6.15pm. Lafferty did not reply to either charge. The same officer also charged McElroy, eight minutes later. McElroy, from Ballymena, made no reply to the importation charge. He replied: 'I know nothing about it', to the possession charge. Det Gda John Madden, of the Ennis drugs unit, said he charged and cautioned Kelly, from Aston, in Birmingham, at 5.40pm in Ennis station. Like Lafferty, he made no reply.

Lafferty and McElroy both had the same solicitor, Gearóid Williams. Mr Williams said he understood his clients had no financial means, and money found on them amounted to very little. He said the State had a duty to provide representation for them because the charges were serious and the men's liberty was at stake. He said a relative would put up substantial bail for McElroy. Superintendent Gerry Kelly said the State objected to bail being granted to Lafferty, McElroy and Kelly. He was heading up the investigation with Chief Superintendent Michael Carty of Ennis and Superintendent Pat Diggin of Ennistymon.

Addressing Judge Mangan, Lafferty said he had one child, and was married but separated. He was unemployed at the time but fishing was his normal employment. He claimed the only money he had was £500. He said he owned no property and had no other assets. The last time he drew unemployment money from the State was the previous March, and he earned about £300 a week when fishing. He replied to Superintendent Kelly that he had no access to money. He had just £8 on him when he was arrested.

McElroy told the court that he was married with five children. He was quoted in the Cork Examiner as saying, 'not quite separated and not quite living with my wife'. He lived in Ballymena, where he was a self-employed steel erector. He said he had not worked for about three months and typically would make £450 a week after tax. He also said he had no assets, bank account or property. He had no funds for a defence team. He said he had gone to Gibraltar to bring a boat home to Ireland.

For his part, Kelly said he had been unemployed for about two months. He had worked as a plasterer and labourer, and typically earned £250 after tax per week.

The men were scheduled to appear before Ennis District Court, exactly a week on from the seizure on board the *Plongeur Wisky*. By then, Gardaí and customs officers in Ireland were taken up with a second unrelated case, after a vessel called the *Tia* was detained in Castletownbere. Four men had been arrested in that operation, also on suspicion of smuggling drugs.

At the Ennis hearing, an application was again made for bail. Once more, the State objected, with Superintendent Gerry Kelly stressing that Lafferty was a risk, as he had lived outside Ireland for a considerable amount of time, and did not have a marriage tie to Ireland because he was separated from his wife. He also explained that Lafferty had signed a document in Gibraltar, the previous month, which gave an address in Manchester. Lafferty's solicitor told the court that his client had lived all of his life in Donegal, apart from three months. However, the bail bid failed and Lafferty was remanded in continuing custody, along with his co-accused.

Officers began working on the Book of Evidence for the trial and were also in contact with their counterparts in Donegal, and across the border with the RUC. It had become evident that the *Plongeur Wisky* had been used in a bid to smuggle drugs into Northern Ireland, possibly for transfer to Britain. Investigations into the purchase of the cabin cruiser in Gibraltar had led police to a network in Northern Ireland.

Just five months after the seizure in Cappagh Pier, the trial of Lafferty, Kelly and McElroy was scheduled to get underway on 22 April. However, when the case came before Ennis Circuit Court, the expected trial did not get underway. The State had entered a *nolle prosequi* on all charges previously brought before Kelly and McElroy. The two relieved men were told they were free to go by the presiding judge, Olive Buttimer.

Lafferty had made a decision about the charges facing him – he opted to plead guilty and was sentenced to six years in prison.

Before the sentencing, the court was told that the vessel had come from Gibraltar and it was believed the intended destination for the consignment was Killybegs. During the investigation, members of the team had been sent to Gibraltar to carry out enquiries. Superintendent Gerry Kelly said he was satisfied there were larger figures in the overall case, but that Lafferty was a very key person because of his role as skipper. He said: 'It is my opinion that the boat was headed for the mainland of England and Scotland.' He believed the cannabis would be either landed on shore or be met by another vessel off Donegal. Also addressing the court, Lafferty's senior counsel, Anthony Sammon, said his client had deep regret and remorse for his involvement in the operation.

Now that the case was over, efforts were made to sell off the *Plongeur Wisky* by the Irish State. It was auctioned by the Revenue Commissioners in Kilrush on 25 June 1997. The vessel was ten years old and had been registered in Nantes. It provided sleeping accommodation for six people. The cabin cruiser was sold for £45,000 to Balbriggan businessman Desmond Quigley. It was renamed *Southern Comfort*.

Although the operation was over in the Republic, a major drive was underway, in Northern Ireland, to target those behind the consignment on board the *Plongeur Wisky*. Two months after Lafferty had been sentenced, an English-born US citizen was brought before Belfast Magistrate's Court on a charge relating to the Clare seizure. Derek Jones from Bally-mena, was charged with inducing another person to import, and possess cannabis resin between September and November 1996. He also faced two charges of money laundering, in rela-tion to allegations that he concealed cash which was the pro-ceeds of crime between December 1995 and June 1997. At the court hearing, Det Constable John Horan of the RUC Serious Crime Squad said 'substantial documentary evidence removed from property belonging to the defendant and busi-nesses relating to him' was the nature of the evidence in the case. Jones was remanded in custody as investigations went on.

During an operation set up to target Jones in relation to money laundering, the paper trail springing from the Clare seizure had also led to the Magherafelt businessman Colin Lees. He was a businessman, who was the managing director of a company called the Lees Group. He had been praised by politicians, like John Hume, for creating employment in Derry during the Troubles. Among his achievements was the development of a shopping centre in Magherafelt. He also had plans to develop a wood pulp factory in Derry. However, his business collapsed in 1992 with debts of £35 million.

Until now, there had not been anything to connect him with drug smuggling but investigations into the *Plongeur Wisky* saga had led police to his door. He was arrested in October 1997 and charged in connection with the Kilrush seizure. The charge arising out of that investigation was inducing others to illegally import cannabis resin into County Clare. At Belfast Magistrates Court, Det Constable John Horan said: 'We have information to suggest that the person behind the importation is the defendant, Colin Lees.'

However, the drugs charge was not the only one facing him. He was charged with smuggling 19,000 cases of spirits into Dover in May 1997, on which duty of stg £770,000 had not been paid. He was also accused of two counts of laundering the proceeds of crime. He and Jones, would be going through the legal system together.

It was now full steam ahead for the RUC in their investigations into the Kilrush drug seizures. Early the following year, one of the five men arrested in Malin Head was charged in connection with it as well. He was car dealer James Millar from Toome Road in Ballymena. He was charged with assisting or inducing others to smuggle the cannabis. His solicitor said his client denied the charge and he applied for bail. The application was opposed and he was remanded in custody. When the case came to court, he received a three-year sentence, which was suspended.

In May 2001 another of the Malin Head group, Ian Symington, also walked free after being given a suspended sentence for his role. The Surrey man appeared in court and
pleaded guilty to two charges of aiding and abetting others in
the *Plongeur Wisky* operation. One of the charges related to
aiding and abetting others in importation, while the other
related to aiding and assisting others in the possession of a
controlled drug for sale or supply. Mr Justice Gillen said he
accepted that the role played by Symington was at the lowest
end of the scale – he had been treated on a 'need to know basis'
and did not know the full extent of the plan. He said: 'Your
case is wholly distinguishable from others who planned,
orchestrated and carried out an obviously sophisticated operation, and I have been persuaded that a wholly exceptional
course can be taken.' As a result, Symington was given two
concurrent two-year sentences, which were suspended.

They were not the only two of the Donegal five to be
charged. Samuel Adams had also been arrested and charged.
He appeared in court on 30 September 1999, alongside Colin
Lees. He pleaded guilty to possessing 1.7 tonnes of cannabis
resin in the Republic for sale or supply between 1 September
and 2 November 1996 at Belfast Crown Court. He also
pleaded guilty to importing the drugs between the same dates.
Adams was given a four-year sentence.

At the same hearing, Lees also pleaded guilty to the two

charges. At that stage, he was already waiting sentencing for fraud and theft charges of £20 million, from his own company, and to involvement in a £2 million drinks scam, where customs and excise were defrauded of duty and VAT on thousands of cases of vodka, whiskey, beer and wine, between October 1996 and June 1997. He had pleaded guilty, in April, to more than forty charges relating to the theft and fraud involving his own company, on dates between 1986 and 1991. He had pleaded guilty to nineteen charges arising out of the drinks scam, earlier that September. The scam involved the buying of alcohol from bonded warehouses in London and Germany that were meant for export to the Republic. The court was told the drink never arrived in the Republic and was instead sold off in Northern Ireland and in the north of England.

Two days after Lees pleaded guilty to the drinks scam on 7 September 1999, Jones went on trial charged with nineteen offences relating to the same events. On 29 September, he was acquitted of eight charges while the jury could not reach agreement on the other eleven. Ten days later, Jones was back in court again, facing trail for the Clare drug seizure. He was acquitted on 27 October. However, he still faced a retrial on the drinks scam because of the hung jury. He also faced a full trial on money laundering charges, so a reporting ban was imposed by the trial judge. When the cases came before the court in December of that year, Jones was given two suspended sentences of four and five years. Effectively, he was a free man.

This all took place as Lees remained in custody, awaiting sentencing for the drinks scam, the drug smuggling and the theft and fraud charges. After Jones's release, Lees hired a new legal team. Knowing the outcome of Jones's case made the businessman want to know if he too could walk free, despite having pleaded guilty. He successfully applied to the High Court to set aside his earlier pleas and allow him to profess his innocence. A six-week trial followed in October 2000 and he was convicted of possession and smuggling the cannabis into Clare. On 30 November 2000 Lees was sentenced to twelve years in prison by Belfast Crown Court for the drugs offences. The forty-eight-year-old had claimed he had been unwittingly used by others to help smuggle £16 million worth of cannabis into the republic. Mr Justice Gillen praised the work of the Irish customs service for their vigilance, and the Gardaí and police for their painstaking work. He said that without their efforts, the pernicious operation might have gone undetected. He said that while others had provided the financial backing for the operation, Lees had been at the heart of the matter, directing and orchestrating operations and organising the purchase of the boat to carry the drugs.

The drugs charges were not the only ones he was facing jail

for. He was also sentenced to between three and nine years, after he pleaded guilty to charges relating to stealing and defrauding from his company. The charges also related to the drinks scam, and a new set of charges relating to money laundering. Mr Justice Gillen told Lees he was a 'man who has not allowed the fear of consequences for yourself, for your family, or the knowledge of the financial havoc you could wreak on others, or even arrest, to deter you.' A reporting restriction was put on the outcome of the case because it was subject to an appeal. The reporting ban was lifted in October 2002, after plans for appeals were abandoned. Although Lees had been given a twelve-year sentence, there was only a year left before he would be freed again, having served half of his sentence. He had been in custody since October 1997.

As expected, he was released from prison in October 2003. However, he was in trouble again just over a year later – this time in England. On 16 November 2004 he was arrested in his home town in a joint operation between the PSNI drugs squad and Merseyside police. Once more, the investigation centred on drug trafficking. He was charged two days later with conspiracy to supply controlled drugs – ecstasy and amphetamines. He appeared at Liverpool City's Magistrates Court, accused of conspiring to supply £31 million of the drugs in Rochdale, in Lancashire. The drugs included 470,000 ecstasy tablets, 9kg (22lb) of MDMA powder, 59kg

(132lb) of amphetamine powder and 20kg (44lb) of amphetamine paste. Once considered an economic saviour to those affected by the Troubles in Derry, the former business-man was once again at the mercy of the justice system because of his involvement in the illegal drugs trade. A second man, Peter Giannasi of West Derby in Liverpool and with an address in Surrey, was also charged in relation to the investigation.

On 31 August the following year, Lees was sentenced to twenty-five years in prison for plotting to supply ecstasy, and a concurrent thirteen-year sentence for a similar charge relating to amphetamine. Giannasi was given seventeen and thirteen-year concurrent sentences. The case came after surveillance was placed on a business unit in Rochdale, where drugs were smuggled in from the Netherlands. The drugs were concealed in pallets of denim jeans.

Passing sentence on the Magherafelt man, Judge John Roberts said Lees visited the Rochdale unit and identified the premises as an ideal staging post for drugs from the Netherlands. According to *The Irish Times*, the judge said: 'I view you as a major player in both conspiracies.' He added: 'You visited that country and you organised delivery of the drugs. I'm prepared to accept there may have been somebody higher up than you in the hierarchy – the banker. Although I view you as being very near the top, I'm prepared to accept that you weren't at the very top of the hierarchy.'

Addressing Giannasi, he said: 'Although you are by no means a Mr Big, you nevertheless played a significant role and in my view you were Colin Lees's right hand man.' He continued: 'Had the drugs come into the country, they would have done enormous harm to the people taking them and would have generated massive profits for those involved with supplying them. Fortunately, they did not.'

After the case, the head of the PSNI's drug squad, Hayden Bell, wholeheartedly welcomed the sentence passed on to Lees. He said: 'We are delighted with the sentence passed today in Liverpool to Colin Lees which brings to a conclusion a major joint PSNI Drugs Squad and Merseyside Police investigation targeting those intent on bringing drugs into the UK and Northern Ireland. The tough sentence reflects the seriousness of the charges for which Colin Lees was convicted. The operation showed the determination of the Law Enforcement Agencies to take top level drugs operators from our streets. As a result of our operation, a major criminal enterprise centring on local, national and international drugs distribution has been broken up. Operations such as this are intelligence-led, pro-active and require great determination and skill, they are protracted and highly resource intensive. These convictions today have prevented millions of pounds worth of drugs destined for consumption in Great Britain and

Northern Ireland. We have removed from circulation millions of pounds of drugs money which has not gone into the pockets of callous drug dealers at every level. This is part of the ongoing PSNI's Organised Crime Branch's priority to put in place major operations to disrupt and convict those responsible for serious criminal activity including importing drugs into the province.'

A negative spotlight had been shone on the dealings of Colin Lees following the arrival of the *Plongeur Wisky* into County Clare in November 1996. The days when he had provided employment for those affected by the Troubles in Northern Ireland seemed very distant when he was convicted in the UK.

Chapter 9

TIA

The waves lashed off the side of the *Tia*, as its skipper sat alone in his cabin. Sigurdur Arngrimsson was eating his evening meal, listening to the tumultuous waves outside. He was looking forward to pulling into the safety of the fishing port of Castletownbere, for a break from the treacherous seas.

It was Tuesday, 5 November 1996 and the weather conditions were terrifying on the open sea. It was not just his own safety he had to think about. He had three crew members on board the massive ship. Even though it was only 9.00pm, they had retired to their cabins and were possibly even asleep by now. They were frustrated after travelling to Surinam on a wasted journey. A cargo planned for Ireland, which included timber, had failed to materialise. It had been bound for Gweedore and the men had hoped to arrive shortly in Rathmullen in Donegal. However, the weather and a damaged rudder on the *Tia* forced them to change course and sail into Castletownbere.

The coaster was now in Castletownbere Sound, near Bere

Island. The safe haven of the fishing port was facing them. However, their voyage into the waters of West Cork had not gone unnoticed and the Irish authorities were anxiously waiting to search the distinctive *Tia*. Confidential information had been received that the vessel was en route to Ireland from South America on a suspected drugs run. Authorities in Ireland had been informed that there was no formal cargo on board and that the coaster had stopped off in the Azores during the long journey. It left there on 29 October to travel towards Ireland. Four days after the successful seizure of 1.7 tonnes of cannabis resin on board the *Plongeur Wisky* cruiser in Clare, the authorities were hoping for another success in Castletownbere.

The navy had been tasked to keep a look out for the *Tia* and had been patrolling the area for the previous four days. They had been alerted about the suspect vessel by the Gardaí. Prior to the 2006 Criminal Justice Act, the navy did not have powers of arrest at sea. They acted, instead, as an aid to the civil power of Gardaí and customs in the joint taskforce on drug interdiction, which had been set up between the three agencies.

The *LE Deirdre* vessel was just leaving its anchorage off Lawrence Cove, on Bere Island, when the *Tia* arrived into the harbour, at the other side of the island. Customs officers in the area had seen the arrival of the vessel and an operation was put into place immediately. While Sigurdur Arngrimsson sat alone eating his evening meal, the naval vessel the *LE Deirdre* had arrived nearby, carrying an armed boarding party from the Irish law enforcement agencies. The lights were off and the naval team did not communicate through its radio, to ensure the *Tia*'s crew would not be aware of the other ship's presence.

Winds at sea were gale force 9 and the captain of the naval vessel, Lieutenant Commander Brian Hevers, had serious reservations about the task the boarding party were about to undertake. Part of the process involved leaving the safety of the naval vessel and sailing to the *Tia* on two rigid inflatable boats. The high seas presented a big risk to the men's safety and Lieutenant Commander Hevers was in regular contact with the commander of naval fleet operations, Commander Eugene Ryan, back on land for direction. Eventually, it was decided to go ahead with the plan and Lieutenant Martin McGrath was the leader of the boarding party, who left the naval vessel to get into the smaller rigid boats. The armed navy man was joined by Detective Sergeant Sean Healy at the helm of the team that had been picked for the operation.

The weather and the sheer size of the ship presented the two men with a major difficulty in getting on board. Because the ship stood tall over their boats, jumping on board was not an option. They tried to attach a ladder to the ship with a grapple and hook, but could not get it secured to the *Tia*.

After several attempts, it looked as if the plan had failed and the ribs left the side of the coaster to return to the *LE Deirdre*. However, members of the boarding party spotted a line hanging over the side of the ship as they made their way back towards the naval vessel. The line was tied to a fender which was attached to the *Tia*. They decided to give the operation another go. Lieutentant McGrath and Detective Sergeant Healy climbed up the line, putting hand over hand in what was a physically exhausting exercise. The next step was to decide whether to search the huge vessel for its crew or help the remaining party members to get on board. They threw a ladder down the side of the ship to their colleagues and hurriedly went to search the vessel themselves. Time was of the essence – they could not afford to give those on board a chance to prepare for their arrival. The element of surprise could prove a powerful weapon if there were drugs on board.

The two armed men first went to the bridge of the coaster. Given the treacherous weather conditions, they expected that at least one member of the crew would be in this area, to keep an eye on the ship's course in the high seas. However, they had met none of the crew members by the time their colleagues joined them, one by one, on the *Tia's* bridge. The lights on the vessel were off, but the team managed to find their way through the ship. They found the captain's cabin first and Sigurdur Arngrimsson's moments of contemplation were interrupted, when they entered and found him having his evening meal. Despite his protestations, he was taken to the bridge while the search of the vessel continued.

The sixty-five-year-old Icelandic captain confirmed he was not travelling alone, and said there were three other crew members on board. The team went first to a cabin in which an African man was sleeping. When he woke up and saw the strangers in his apartment, he became terrified and shouted at the armed men. An Englishman was found in another cabin, and it was obvious that he had not been aware of their presence on board either. However, when the team reached the third cabin, the Irishman who had been sleeping there had been woken up by the commotion. He was sitting up in bed when they entered his cabin. It later emerged he was from Youghal, in County Cork, and was named John O'Shea.

The *Tia* was brought into the harbour and O'Shea, the African and the Englishman were all arrested by Gardaí. Arngrimsson was allowed remain on board to help move the *Tia* to a jetty at Dinish Island, the day after the ship was detained by the boarding party. The island is joined to the mainland by a bridge and located across the port from the local fishing fleet. When the vessel was moved, the skipper was also arrested. As the four men were being questioned by Gardaí in Bandon and Castletownbere, two men were also being held in Dublin in connection with the ship's arrival in Irish territorial waters. One of them was also an Icelandic native, who was living in Dublin at the time. All six were being held under new drug trafficking legislation. The Criminal Justice Drug Trafficking Act 1996 had come into effect in September of that year, just months after the murders of Detective Garda Jerry McCabe and *Sunday Independent* crime correspondent Veronica Guerin. Even though the Act had been going through the Dáil since the spring, the killings had led to a moral outrage in Ireland and resulted in the bill being pushed through as quickly as possible. The new Act had given stronger powers to Gardaí in relation to the detention of prisoners, allowing suspects to be held for up to seven days without charge. Until then, suspects could only be held for twelve hours.

Investigators enlisted the help of Interpol to carry out enquiries abroad, particularly in Iceland and South America. The investigation was also extended to Sweden, where Arngrimsson, a former Lutheran minister, had an address in Malmo. While the focus of the investigation became international, an intricate search was being carried out on the ship by customs rummage experts and a Garda forensics team. There was no immediate sign of drugs on the vessel and the search teams carried out minute examinations of every part of the boat. Every water and oil tank was emptied and the cargo holds were also searched. The interior panelling and air vents were dismantled, but there was still no evidence of drugs on board.

The search then switched to the ballast tanks, in the hold of the ship, and it became clear that this area had been tampered with. There was evidence of fresh welding in the area and the rummage teams were hoping that this was where the suspected consignment of drugs would be hidden. Cutting equipment was brought in and a number of steel panels were removed. However, nothing was found – despite the intensive search.

With no drugs found on board, so far, investigators felt it was essential that the crew be held longer for questioning. An application was made to extend the period of detention for Arngrimsson at a sitting of Bantry District Court on 8 November, two days after he was arrested. Chief Superintendent Noel Smith made the application to Judge Con O'Leary under the Criminal Justice Act. Chief Supt Smith said the search of the *Tia* was a complicated and detailed exercise. He said the team faced the risk of escaping gases and were working on a ship that was in bad condition. The judge granted the extension of seventy-two hours.

Before the application was granted, the court heard from Arngrimsson, who went in to the witness box to deny that the *Tia* had ever been used in connection with drug smuggling. He said: 'There's no drugs, to my knowledge, on the ship.' He said he had brought the vessel to South America to collect timber, but the cargo never materialised. He said a 'gentleman's agreement' followed with an unnamed party in South America, and on 8 October he headed for the Azores, where the ballast tanks were re-welded. The skipper said the *Tia* encountered steering difficulties off the Irish coast, with the automatic steering system breaking down and the manual system also failing. He was having his supper on board the ship, off the Fastnet Rock, on the night the boarding party climbed on the *Tia*. He said he was taken to the bridge of the boat at gunpoint, and that he was arrested and handcuffed. He said: 'Another man pointed a pistol at me for more than a half hour.' Arngrimsson told the court that he was then taken to the cabin for questioning and that he had been under 'arrest' until 1.30am the following morning. The State's position was that none of the four had been arrested until later that day.

The application in Cork was echoed by a similar application in Dublin, where Gardaí were continuing to question the two men arrested there. Another man had also been arrested in Cork city in connection with the investigation. That man was known to drug squad Gardaí, in the broader Cork area. He was suspected of having played a pivotal role at a local level in the *Tia* operation. However, he was later released without charge. The focus of the investigation had now become national, spearheaded by the Garda National Drugs Unit, under Detective Chief Superintendent Kevin Carty. Because of the national perspective, the incident room for the case was located in Kells, in Meath, a central location to make it easier for Gardaí to collate the happenings in Cork and Dublin with investigations in Donegal, where the *Tia* had planned to arrive in Ireland.

The searchers on board the *Tia* continued their work but eventually had to concede that the expected haul of cocaine would not materialise. The armed protection around the boat was stood down on 12 November and the *Tia* was handed over to the responsibility of Colm Harrington from Bere Island to act as agent of the boat, while Arngrimsson was in custody. Meanwhile, two days after the extra time was granted, the Englishman and the African were released without charge. They both flew to London following their ordeal, happy to be free. However, Arngrimsson and O'Shea remained in custody until the following day. They were released without charge later that evening.

The nightmare was not over yet. Their investigations convinced case officers that there had been a plan to smuggle drugs on board the *Tia* from South America to Europe. As a result, the focus of the investigation had turned to the issue of conspiracy to import cocaine. As Arngrimsson was enjoying his first taste of freedom in almost a week, Gardaí were preparing to re-arrest him. He had gone to a pub in Bandon town after his release and was arrested there at 7.00pm that evening. He was taken back to the local Garda Station, where he was charged with conspiring to import cocaine into Ireland between 8 August and 5 November. He was released on his own bail of £20,000 two weeks later. According to *The Irish Times*, the delay was caused because Arngrimsson's brother, Josefat, was refused as a bondsman by Judge Brendan Wallace, after he was heard in court that he had two convictions for fraud. His solicitor, Ray Hennessy, told the court at that hearing on 19 November that Sigurdur Arngrimsson was willing to sell the *Tia*. The vessel had been valued at £125,000. Judge Wallace made it a condition of his bail that the bond would be deducted from the sale of the vessel, during a hearing two months later when he reduced the bond to £5,000.

A file was prepared and sent forward to the DPP. He recommended that O'Shea also be charged for his role in the *Tia* operation. In 6 May 1997 a warrant was obtained from Judge Wallace in Bandon District Court. He was arrested in Youghal, on 6 May, and charged with conspiracy to import drugs into Ireland between 1 July and 5 November 1996. He was brought before a special sitting of the court in Bandon that evening at 6.45pm and released on his own bail bond.

In February 1998, nine months later, the conspiracy cases came to trial at Cork Circuit Criminal Court. Arngrimsson went on trial by himself. O'Shea's case was not put to the jury because he opted to plead guilty before the trial started. Because Arngrimsson had yet to go on trial, an order was made preventing the media reporting the development.

In a statement to Gardaí after his initial arrest, the Youghal man said a friend of his had gotten in touch in July of that year and told him there was a job on a boat run for timber. He was told the job would take about two months. In the statement to Detective Sergeant Martin Sullivan, O'Shea said his friend had told him to meet the *Tia* in Totness, in England, and that he did so in August. He said he met a man called Ziggy during that trip and Ziggy told him they would be going to the Netherlands for a cargo of timber. However, Ziggy later told him there was a change of plan and that the *Tia* would be sailing to Surinam. The trip to South America took eighteen days, with a stop off in Las Palmas on the way. The crew spent a month in Surinam waiting for cargo. In that statement, he denied knowing about the plans to bring drugs to Europe on board the *Tia* and said he got suspicious when it returned to Ireland without cargo. O'Shea told Detective Sergeant Sullivan that he had been given £1,000 for his work, as a cook, on the *Tia* and that he had spent most of it on drink and women.

However, he revealed more in a later statement. He outlined how his friend had told him in July before travelling to the Netherlands that they would first meet with figures from

Dublin. He described them as 'serious people, the cream of drugs'. He continued: 'I was to make sure that that the drugs were put safely on board. A few days before I went to Holland, I was contacted by two men in a café in Youghal. One man told me that this was going to be the biggest load of drugs that ever came to Ireland. He said that once I got back safely with the drugs, I would never again have to worry about money. He did not mention a sum but I knew that it would be big considering that I had been given £4,000 last year for just organising a trawler.'

In an earlier statement made by Barry Clohessy from Youghal, Gardaí were told that he had been approached by O'Shea, before Christmas 1995, about getting access to a trawler. According to Mr Clohessy, O'Shea told him that he had friends who wanted the use of a trawler to go out to sea to collect duty free items. Mr Clohessy worked as a skipper on a trawler at the time. He alleged: 'A couple of days before Christmas, John O'Shea gave me a bundle of money. I asked him what it was for and he said: "To have a drink for Christmas".' A few weeks later, O'Shea arranged to meet Mr Clohessy in a pub in Killeagh, in East Cork, and introduced him to two friends of his. One of the strangers asked the Youghal trawler skipper if he had agreed to bring some drums or barrels in from sea. Mr Clohessy told Gardaí the man had told him during the meeting that he would look after him financially.

However, Mr Clohessy said his boss had said he did not want anything to do with the job if it was connected to drugs. The man called to Mr Clohessy the following summer and was looking for O'Shea. He was the man who was later arrested in Cork city by officers investigating the arrival of the *Tia* into Castletownbere.

During the Garda investigation, two tickets for flights from Cork to Amsterdam had been unearthed. The tickets were in the names of O'Shea and the man arrested in Cork city. A receipt from the company which had supplied the tickets revealed that £734 had been paid to the holiday company on 12 July 1996.

According to O'Shea's second statement, a contact of his involved in the drugs run had told him he had invested £35,000 in the operation. O'Shea continued: 'When I went to Amsterdam, my contact introduced me to another person around fifty years of age. He said it was going to be the biggest load of drugs ever brought into Ireland. My contact flew back to Ireland the following day and I stayed in Amsterdam for some time.' The five-man crew was assembled for the journey to Surinam and included Arngrimsson, as the skipper, and another man called Yoop.

O'Shea told Gardaí how two other crewmen, called Richard and Sunday, had been sent off the vessel while preparations were made to bring the drugs on board. This was about two weeks after the crew had arrived in Surinam. The main aim was to identify somewhere on board to hide the cargo and holes were cut into the hull, after it was decided that this area was the safest location. He said Yoop went on shore one day and returned to tell him that drugs would be brought on board the *Tia* that night. As a result, Sunday and Richard were to be sent on shore again, so that they would not see the contraband being brought onto the vessel. However, the plans received a major setback. The drugs did not arrive that night, and Yoop and another man went to check out the situation onshore the following day. They returned with the news that the crew would have to wait another few days.

O'Shea said he was told that those in charge of the operation onshore had 'fucked up' and that it was decided to wait the extra days, to see if the plan could be salvaged. The Youghal man went ashore one evening before the crew left for Europe. He related to Gardaí how a new problem had emerged when he returned to the ship. He explained: 'When I came back to the boat at around 4.00am, there was an almighty row going on in the captain's cabin. They were shouting and roaring at each other in a foreign language but I did not see who was there.' According to O'Shea, checks later that morning revealed that the drugs, which were scheduled to be brought on board the *Tia*, were still on the outskirts of the town and that the people who were to transfer them to the crew were looking for more money.

Frustrated with the delay, a decision was taken to head back to Europe – without the drugs and the cargo of timber. The vessel headed for the Azores, where welding was done to cover up the holes that had been made to provide hiding places for the drugs. Food and water for the remainder of the journey to Rathmullen were also brought on board, during the four days they spent in the Azores. The men now just wanted to go home and forget about the whole disastrous journey. However, the nightmare continued when the weather worsened and a rudder on the *Tia* was damaged, as the vessel edged closer to Ireland. This in turn led to the court case in which Arngrimsson now found himself alone, after O'Shea's decision to plead guilty.

When the Icelandic man's trial for conspiracy got underway, the court was told by prosecuting Senior Counsel Ralph Sutton that the charge related to when two or more people combined to do something unlawful. He said there was evidence that Arngrimsson had combined with others to import cocaine into Ireland. He alleged that the former minister had ordered that openings be made in the ballast tanks, under the cargo hold, while he was in South America. According to *The Irish Times*, he said: 'There will be evidence there was ample space in this area to accommodate the storage of drugs and you will also have evidence that there was considerable talk about drugs being loaded on board the ship.' He added: 'The fact that he never carried the drugs and that he never brought the drugs in is immaterial. The fact that he planned to do so is a serious offence.'

Detective Sergeant Maurice Walsh gave evidence of arresting Arngrimsson in Castletownbere after he had helped bring the *Tia* into the port town. He said the Irish authorities were acting on confidential information that the skipper was involved in drug trafficking from South America to Ireland. He also said the authorities were aware that alterations had been carried out to his ship that were not justified and that the ship had travelled an unusually long journey without a cargo.

The case was a complex one, unusual in its nature given that no drugs had been found on board the vessel. After the prosecution's case was outlined, legal argument dominated the proceedings for close to three days. The twelve-member jury were sent from the courtroom while this took place, eliminating the possibility of them hearing anything which would influence their verdict on whether or not the Icelandic had conspired to import cocaine from South America. However, the decision was taken out of their hands when they returned to the courtroom on 13 February. The presiding judge, AG Murphy, directed the jury to find the accused man not guilty, explaining his decision by saying: 'For legal reasons, the trial cannot continue.'

Arngrimsson's detention after Gardaí and customs became aware that no drugs were on board the *Tia* was the issue which determined Judge Murphy's course of action.

A submission had been made during legal argument by defence Senior Counsel Ciarán O'Loughlin in relation to the detention. He argued that Arngrimsson had been unlawfully held by Gardaí. The main plank of his argument was that his client should have been released at 1.00pm on 9 November, four days after his arrest under the drug trafficking act.

Judge Murphy agreed with the argument and ruled: 'That was not done and anything else that emerged afterwards was inadmissible.'

Sitting in the courtroom, Arngrimsson breathed a sigh of relief. However, O'Shea's decision to plead guilty to the conspiracy charge had to be dealt with before the *Tia*'s skipper could go and celebrate the turn of events. O'Shea had been a part-time fisherman and had been working as a cook on board the *Tia*. Detective Sergeant Sean Healy told Judge Murphy that the Youghal man was a small cog in a much bigger machine. The judge said that the charge was a serious one which would normally attract a heavy penalty. However, he acknowledged the view of Gardaí that O'Shea had tried to back out of the operation, but was forced to continue by other individuals. He said: 'This man was unintelligent enough to accept favours from people who used him.' He handed down a ten-year sentence, which he suspended.

Once the case was over, the media attention turned to the skipper. He said (outside the court) that O'Shea's decision to plead guilty had caused him to worry about the outcome of his own trial. The end of the case came a day after the sixth anniversary of his wife's death. The skipper had spent the week in a guesthouse in Cork city, where he believed the spirits of his wife and dead mother had been with him during the tough days of his trial. He explained: 'My mother used to feed stray cats. The woman there (in the guesthouse) was feeding stray cats too. I knew from that that my mother was with me in spirit.' The former Lutheran minister also said he could feel God's presence with him. He said: 'When I felt alone during the trial I thought of God. He was with me today. I am hugely relieved by the result. It has restored my faith in the Irish legal profession and system.' He added: 'Anything whatsoever to do with drugs is against all my beliefs and I asserted my innocence right from the beginning.'

The saga of the *Tia*'s arrival into Castletownbere in November 1996 had come to an end. Because no drugs were found on board the vessel, the *Tia* was not confiscated by the State and remained in Arngrimsson's ownership after the trial. Despite fourteen arrests across the country, nobody has ever served time in prison in connection with the case. However, at least one person suspected of involvement with the operation fled Ireland after the establishment of the Criminal Assets Bureau, set up in 1996 to target assets gained through criminality. Sources suggest that intelligence gathering identified a Dublin man as the principal operator behind the scenes, but there was insufficient evidence to bring him to court for the *Tia* conspiracy.

Chapter 10

POSIDONIA

As the Fastnet Rock, off Ireland's southwest coast, came into view, the three crew members on board the *MV Posidonia* were in a celebratory mood. They had travelled thousands of kilometres by sea from the northern tip of Africa to the southern tip of Ireland, and their destination was now staring them in the face.

The Fastnet Rock and its lighthouse had become known as the 'Teardrop of Ireland' to generations of people, who had left Ireland to start a new life in America. It was the last view of their native land for the thousands of emigrants, who had sailed from Cobh, formerly known as Queenstown. For Britons Richard George Preece, Matthew Simpkins and Barry Court, the Fastnet could not have been more welcome as they came near to the Irish coast on board the British-registered *Posidonia* in November 1999. They had sailed from Morocco with precious cargo on a trip which was set to earn them thousands of pounds each. The only tears they were expecting to shed on seeing the Fastnet Rock were ones of joy.

Court and Simpkins were now within days of having their dreams of wealth come true, thanks to Preece. The Hertfordshire native was the link between them and the mission they were carrying out. If fate had not intervened in Preece's life and taken him to work in a boatyard in Gibraltar, none of them would be travelling in a converted fishing trawler, off the coast of Ireland. Life had thrown up a mixed bag for Preece. The former British Army man had also worked as a teacher, before leaving the UK to live in Spain and Portugal. He set up a ferry business but that failed a short few years later, in the mid 1990s. It was time, once more, to try something different, so he moved to Gibraltar, where he was employed in a boatyard, skippering vessels. However, he had run into difficulties again and claimed to Gardaí that a meeting with two Dutchmen in December 1998 changed the course of his life. This was the moment when Preece faced a moral dilemma. His change of circumstances changed his mind about the possibility of making a living from an illegal trade.

Of that first meeting, he later claimed he went to a café on the waterfront in Gibraltar, where he enjoyed a few beers with the two men. He said they asked him if he was interested in taking part in a drugs run, delivering up to 2 tonnes of cannabis to the Netherlands. Preece said he refused the invitation at that first meeting. However, within months he changed his mind. The following June, he agreed to become involved in a plan to deliver cannabis to Ireland. Although he told Gardaí initially that the cannabis was destined for the Netherlands, he subsequently said it was for the Irish market, casting doubt about possible Dutch involvement in the operation. It is believed that a major gang in Ireland were behind the importation attempt, although nobody from the Irish side of the operation has ever been charged in connection with it.

Sticking to his story about the involvement of the two Dutchmen, Preece claimed they gave him £42,000 to purchase a vessel for the trip. Preece located the *Posidonia* and bought it at the end of September. Originally called the *Humber Pioneer*, the boat had been bought by Cambridge University in 1992 for use on a research project in the Arctic region. It was renamed the *Posidonia* at that point. The boat was being used as a sailing ship in Gibraltar, when Preece came across it and he felt it would be ideal for the smuggling operation. Once the purchase was made, the voyage to Morocco to collect the cannabis started to become a reality. Before it could get underway, crew members had to be recruited. Fellow British expatriate Barry Court was an obvious choice for the trips to Morocco and Ireland. Preece had known him for about three years. Court was an engineer, who had been living in Spain for twenty years. He later said he didn't know Preece very well, until six weeks before the run to Morocco. He was recruited to the operation because of his in-depth knowledge of engines. This was a valuable trait in the event of any mechanical problems arising with the *Posidonia*. Simpkins had been working on a barge in Gibraltar, when he was also recruited to the operation. The Englishman was a former painter and decorator, who had moved to Spain with his family, more than a decade earlier.

Preece stood to gain most from the operation, because of his role as skipper. A sweetener was that he would gain ownership of the boat, once the run was successfully completed. A payment of £38,000 was also included in the package. Court was promised £60,000 for his role, while Simpkins had been told he would be paid £40,000. The men had to carry out the successful run before they would receive the promised payments. Arrangements had been made by the organisers of the operation that the trio would be met 5km off the coast of Morocco, by someone involved in the operation from the African side. The *Irish Examiner* quoted a statement made by Preece weeks later, in which he said: 'We went to the coordinates we were given off the coast of Morocco. This guy who was speaking French very badly directed me in closer to the beach and then appeared a small rubber boat with two guys. I helped load the hash onto my boat.'

Great care was taken in loading bale after bale of cannabis resin on to the *Posidonia*. When the work was finished, 1.5 tonnes had been shifted from one boat to the other. The three

Britons were now ready for the next leg of their journey, with Ireland as the destination. Skipper Preece had been directed to sail to the Fastnet Rock, where the drugs were to be transferred on to another boat. He had been given instructions to await contact by phone or radio, once the *Posidonia* had reached the shipping lane separation zone near the Fastnet Rock. He was told that co-ordinates for a location at sea would be given to him at that point, and that the off-loading of the drugs from the *Posidonia* would take place there.

As the crew made the journey to Ireland, hopes were high. The voyage to Morocco had gone without a hiccup. They did not even have to meet another vessel along the way for a fuel top up, because of the *Posidonia*'s economical engine. Such was the novelty of the responsibility given to them that they decided to record it for posterity. Preece and Simpkins posed on top of the bales, smiling widely at the Polaroid camera. As they neared their destination, the three men were thanking their lucky stars that Preece's choice was going to turn their lives around. Simpkins was busy making plans, in his head, for the money he had been promised. He had a partner and one child, and wanted to make a new life for his family. He hoped that his plans to open a cyber café would happen now that he was involved in this drugs venture.

However, Simpkins and his colleagues had not bargained for the vigilance of a fisherman, who saw the *Posidonia* moving west towards the Fastnet during the afternoon of 16 November. He wondered why the vessel was loitering in the area. His suspicions prompted him to contact the customs office in Bantry to alert them about the boat.

When the call came in to the customs office in Bantry, staff made contact with their regional office in Cork to pass on the information they had received. The fisherman's suspicions were seen as significant, because he had valuable knowledge of regular movements along the local coastline. If he had concerns, they had to be taken seriously. When the call was received in Cork, a decision was taken to alert the navy, who could dispatch a vessel to the area for surveillance. As the *Posidonia*'s crew were looking forward to a proper night's sleep, away from bales of cannabis resin, the navy's *LE Ciara* was on its way to West Cork, commanded by Lieuntenant Commander Martin McGrath.

As the *LE Ciara* edged its way westwards, naval officers on board used a radar system to zone in on the *Posidonia*'s exact location at about 7.30pm that evening. They could immediately see why the vessel had aroused the suspicion of the fisherman. Not alone was it loitering too long in the area but it was also in a blatant state of disrepair, with rust streaks all over it. The officers could see, as well, that the boat was in a location usually used only by fishing vessels and merchant traffic, purposes for which the *Posidonia* was clearly not suitable.

With their suspicions aroused, the naval team then headed to Baltimore to pick up four customs officers. Ready for their mission, the joint team returned to sea to locate the *Posidonia*. The trawler had by now moved nearer to the Fastnet, but was travelling at a slow pace. The task of the navy and customs officers was to ensure it was within 19km of the Irish coast. Under the Maritime Jurisdiction Act 1959, the powers of the customs agency did not extend beyond the 19km zone and its officers on board the naval ship could not legally take part in a boarding of the *Posidonia*, if it had been outside the limit. The team on board the *LE Ciara* prepared for a swoop on the crew of the trawler as night fell. Members of the navy were armed with Browning automatic pistols to protect them and the remainder of the boarding party from any possible attack from those on board the suspect vessel.

The team hoped to surprise the crew when the mission got underway, after 9.00pm. A decision had been taken to blacken out the ship, to prevent it being seen by the occupants of the *Posidonia*. However, Preece, Simpkins and Court had become aware of the *LE Ciara* before it had sailed to Baltimore. Not surprisingly, the news that the navy had arrived in the area prompted panic on board the vessel, as the crew wondered what to do with the consignment of cannabis resin. The *Irish Examiner* quoted Preece as saying: 'We had to change the filter and I had just done that when the patrol boat put its light on us. When the patrol boat left, we discussed throwing the stuff overboard but we decided against that. We discussed where we would go and I wanted to go to Bantry because it was nearer. Before going into Bantry I felt the stuff would be safer under the floor in the wheelhouse. We were in the process of doing that when the patrol boat arrived back.'

They were so busy with this mission that they failed to notice the return of the *LE Ciara*. Two rigid inflatable boats were launched from the naval ship, containing a boarding party of six naval personnel and two customs officers. The members of the boarding party were now in a very vulnerable position, having left the safety of the *LE Ciara*. They were facing into an unknown situation, with no way of establishing if the crew of the *Posidonia* were armed. They also had no idea if those on board knew that a boarding party was preparing to jump onto the boat.

The first to transfer to the trawler was Lieuntenant Brian Fitzgerald, the boarding officer for the operation. He had only joined the *LE Ciara* five days before and was still getting to know the crew. His hopes of an early success in his new post were realised within seconds of boarding the *Posidonia*. He could see through the windows that there were at least three men on board, who obviously had no idea that they had visitors. While his colleagues followed him onto the ship, Lieuntenant Fitzgerald's next priority was to find the entry into the cabin. He checked each door on the ship and found one which had light beaming out from around it. The team of six naval officers entered the cabin, while Commander McGrath made contact with customs, by radio, to ask them to stand by. As the joint party had hoped, the men were totally unprepared for the arrival of the armed party. The members of the boarding party knew the *Posidonia* would join the list of other ships caught with drugs on board in the previous decade. Some of the cannabis had been carried into the wheel-house and an attempt was made to cover some of the bales with tarpaulin. However, much of the haul was plainly visible to the boarding party. Customs officer John O'Sullivan could see four bales of resin in the saloon of the boat. His colleague, Patrick O'Regan, saw a further fourteen bales lying on a bunk on the starboard side of the vessel.

Preece cut an unusual figure in the cabin when it was taken over by the boarding party. Although it was the middle of winter, he wore a t-shirt, jeans and flip flops. His clothing was in sharp contrast to the outfits worn by the boarding party. They were each covered from head to toe, wearing black boots, black helmets, bullet-proof vests, and black gloves. They had by now taken control of the vessel and Preece's role at the helm was over. The *Posidonia* was brought into Schull harbour at 2.45am on 17 November, after officers decided it was more suitable than Cork or Castletownbere. The ship could be brought into a private area of the pier and it was the nearest port to the Fastnet. Gardaí had been alerted about the developments and were waiting on the pier to arrest the three Britons. The three men were then taken to Bandon Garda station, the divisional headquarters for policing in West Cork. As they were being questioned under drug trafficking legislation, the *Posidonia* remained under guard in Schull harbour. Essentially, the boat had become a crime scene – a team from the Garda Technical Bureau travelled from Dublin to carry out a detailed forensics examination of the vessel. Customs officers also carried out their own investigation on board.

During the search, the photographs of Simpkins and Preece, which had been taken in moments of daredevil bonhomie, were found when the investigators came across a bible. The images had been hidden between the pages of the holy book. They were later used as evidence in court to demonstrate that the men had been very aware that there was cannabis on board. In one photograph, a smiling Simpkins was shown giving the thumbs up sign with two gloved hands, sitting on bales of the drug.

One of the critical aspects of the investigation was to establish the men's destination. Investigators also wanted to determine where the men had come from and what route they had followed. As with any drugs shipment, navigational charts on board the *Posidonia* were crucial. Meanwhile, officers in

Bandon were busy questioning the three crew members. Preece made a statement to Gardaí outlining how he had become involved in the botched smuggling effort and told officers that he had been finding it difficult to get a job at the time. His statement of how the operation unfolded was corroborated by statements from Simpkins and Court. However, by the end of the first day of questioning, officers had some concerns that they were not being told the full story. This was because the navigational charts on the vessel contradicted some of Preece's version of events.

He told Gardaí the drugs were bound for the Netherlands, although the *Posidonia* had been heading west instead of east when first spotted by the navy on 16 November. The investigating team wondered why the vessel was headed so close to the Cork coast, if the intended destination was on mainland Europe. The charts on board the vessel had undergone a preliminary examination by a navy navigational expert and he found eight of the most recent charts to be the most important. Of those charts, five related to Irish territorial waters, prompting officers to wonder why this was so, when the Netherlands was supposed to be the intended destination. Of further significance was that two of the charts related particularly to Cork and had detailed maps of Cork harbour. Papers found on the vessel revealed that those charts, along with others detailing approaches to Ireland, had all been purchased on 21 and 22 September, less than two months before the cannabis seizure. The absence of navigational charts for ports in the Netherlands could not be ignored.

Flags flying on the *Posidonia* also provided a vital clue. Three flew from the converted trawler, representing Britain, Spain and Ireland. The absence of the Dutch flag was seen as crucial evidence that the Netherlands was not on the itinerary. All this was backed up by a log book found on board. On the last page of the book, co-ordinates off the Irish coast had been marked in handwriting. A book on yachting was also found on the vessel. It gave details about harbours, rivers and inlets in Ireland. When this combined evidence was put to the men, they eventually agreed that the cannabis, was indeed, destined for the Irish market.

Two days after the men's arrest, all three were taken from Bandon Garda station to the courthouse in Macroom. They were charged on directions from the DPP with possession of the cannabis for sale or supply. They were also charged under the Customs Consolidation Act 1876 with importing and dealing with the drug in Irish territorial waters. The court was told that the three made no reply when charged with the offences. Preece had an address in London, while the other two had addresses in La Linea, Cadiz, in Spain. They had no assets within the Irish state and Judge James O'Connor granted them free legal aid. Their solicitor, Con Murphy, said his clients had no objection to being remanded in custody and the three spent their first night in an Irish prison. They were due to appear in court in Bantry a week later.

The search of the *Posidonia* took a number of days, as the investigation teams tried to ensure all evidence was gathered in their efforts to build a case against the suspects. The vessel itself was not in good repair and the engine room had flooded, after its detention off the Fastnet. Once the search was over, it was removed from Schull and towed to an upriver boatyard near Innishannon, between Bandon and Cork city. It was later taken to Kinsale, where it remained for several months.

Case officers worked solidly on the investigation. Nearly three months later, a further charge – that of importing the drugs into the State between November 14 and 16 – was brought by the DPP. The men were again taken to Macroom courthouse, where the Books of Evidence against them were served. A trial date was set for 15 May at Cork Circuit Criminal Court, which had seen similar major cases in recent years.

Seven men and five women were sworn in to hear the case as Gardaí, and naval and customs officers waited to give evidence on behalf of the prosecution. The jury was told the trial would take up to a week. Preece, Court and Simpkins all pleaded not guilty and placed their fate in the hands of the jury. The possession charge they faced was for the sale or supply of more than £10,000 of the drug. Under Section 15A of the Misuse of Drugs Act, the men faced a mandatory sentence of ten years imprisonment each – if convicted.

However, they would have to wait a while longer to hear their fate. Although the jury selection and the arraignment had gone ahead, there was a delay in hearing the evidence, because of legal argument. In the absence of the jury, it was revealed to the court that the State had not obtained a key document from the then Minister for Foreign Affairs, Brian Cowen, to enable the prosecution of foreign nationals in an Irish court. Under Section 11.1 of the Maritime Jurisdiction Act 1959, proceedings cannot be taken against foreign nationals, who are alleged to have committed offences while on board a foreign ship that has entered Irish waters, without a certificate of clearance from the Minister for Foreign Affairs. There was a glimmer of hope for the three suspects, but the State's team sought an adjournment of the case, until the following morning, in the hope that 'something would turn up' to assist their case.

The jury members were called back to the courtroom at 2.45pm that afternoon, to be updated by Judge AG Murphy. He said: 'Ladies and gentlemen, grave difficulty has arisen in the prosecution of this case through no fault on the part of the accused. I have no choice but to put it back until tomorrow morning.' He did not elaborate on the nature of the 'grave difficulty' and directed the jury to return at 10.40am the following morning.

As the jury went home for the night, they were not prepared for the drama of the following day. When they returned to the courthouse on Camden Quay in Cork City that morning, they were not allowed into the trial courtroom, as the issue of the clearance certificate still had not been remedied. Senior counsel John Edwards said a *nolle prosequi* would be entered in the case, meaning that the men would not be prosecuted and would instead be released from custody. However, he said the men would then be re-charged. Defence counsels Ciarán O'Loughlin SC, Tom Creed SC, Pat McCarthy SC and Siobhán Langford BL all opposed the State's proposal. Mr O'Loughlin argued that the State should not be in a position to enter a *nolle prosequi*, because the case had not been put before the jury. According to the *Irish Examiner's* account of the hearing, Mr McCarthy said: 'There has been an abuse of process and I do not mean to cast aspersions on any individuals. You should put a permanent stay on this indictment. We are in a very exceptional and extraordinary situation in this trial. Undoubtedly it will be the subject of further proceedings. The Director of Public Prosecutions should not be allowed to mend its hand. It is inappropriate'.

Despite the efforts of the defence teams, Judge Murphy told the men at lunchtime that they were free to leave the court. He said: 'The primary duty of the court is to see on behalf of society that justice is done. Everything else is subordinate … I do not have the power to order that the accused in this case be put in charge of the jury. The fact that a *nolle prosequi* is entered prior to the jury being put in charge cannot invalidate a *nolle prosequi*. I find myself bound by that and the practice and history of the matter.'

After being in custody for six months, Preece, Court and Simpkins were released but then re-arrested, outside the courtroom, within minutes of the judge's decision. They were taken back to West Cork, where they appeared before Judge James O'Connor that afternoon at a district court sitting in Clonakilty. There was an element of déjà vu to the hearing, as they were again charged with importing cannabis resin and with possession of the drug for sale or supply in Irish territorial waters on 16 November. Once again, they were granted free legal aid. They were remanded in custody to appear at a remand hearing in Bantry three days later.

State solicitor for West Cork, Malachy Boohig, told the court that the crucial documents of clearance from Minister Brian Cowen had been secured on this occasion. He said the solicitors representing Preece, Court and Simpkins had all been given copies of the certificates. He also said that the Books of Evidence in the case could be served on the men ahead of the next remand hearing

Preece, Court and Simpkins had smelled freedom, for a brief few minutes, in the Cork courthouse, before they were recharged following the aborted trial. Their defence teams had battled hard against a *nolle prosequi* and a decision was taken to mount a legal challenge to the men's on-going detention. While preparations were being made by the State for a new trial, the men's defence teams took their challenge to the High Court. They argued that the State had used unlawful means to detain them when they were first arrested, because the key documents of clearance had not been obtained from Minister Cowen. They sought an order that would prohibit the DPP from continuing legal proceedings against them. Since the necessary certificates were not issued until 16 May, it was argued that the men had been held in unlawful custody before that point.

Representing Simpkins, Tom Creed SC said that the adjournment of the trial on its opening day had given the State the chance to get the necessary documents from the Minister of Foreign Affairs. He argued that the prosecution's side had used unlawful means to secure the detention of the three men until it had regularised its position to allow the State's case to proceed. Six months after the trial was aborted, the way was paved for a new trial to get underway when the men's legal challenge failed.

After so many hurdles, the second trial was scheduled to get underway in the Circuit Criminal Court in Cork on 13 February 2001. Given the men's legal challenge against their detention, it came as little surprise when they pleaded not guilty when they were arraigned. A new jury was selected and it seemed that everything was in order for the trial to proceed. However, the jury was discharged when it emerged that the wrong charges had been put on the indictment. The State's side was now hoping that the third time would prove lucky when the men were re-arraigned and a new jury of nine men and three women were sworn in to hear the case. The trial did go ahead two days later. Judge AG Murphy said the trial could last for weeks instead of days, because of legal debate.

When the trial eventually got underway, the court was told that the prosecution case would be that Preece, Court and Simpkins had crewed the *Posidonia* knowing that the drugs were on board. Prosecution barrister Donal McCarthy said the three defendants must have known because packages containing the cannabis were strewn on the floor of the boat. More packages were stored quite openly at the back of the vessel. This was reiterated by customs officers, John O'Sullivan and Patrick O'Regan, who outlined that they had seen bales in the saloon and on a bunk in the converted trawler, when they boarded it off the Fastnet. The statement made by Preece to Detective Sergeant Gerry McCarthy in Bandon Garda station, explaining how he became involved in the operation, was heard by the jury. Neither Preece, Court nor Simpkins gave evidence during the twelve-day trial.

Closing submissions were made to the court by the prosecution and defence on 27 February. In his closing statement, Mr McCarthy said that an important part of the case was that each of the men had made statements of admission. The statements made by Court and Simpkins to Gardaí in Bandon corroborated the information given by Preece in his statement to Detective Sergeant McCarthy. The barrister said there was evidence by investigating officers that the accused were forthcoming, open and relaxed when they made their statements, a description which he said was the antithesis of being under pressure. Referring to what he called 'corroborative evidence' of sea charts, he said these supported the view that Ireland was the destination for the drugs. He said the equivalent of the Irish Sea road map was on board the *Posidonia*. He reiterated to the jury that the defendants knew there was cannabis on board. He said that even without the statements, the jury also had the evidence surrounding the boarding of the vessel by the navy and customs officers and what they subsequently found. Central to the defence team's closing argument was that the only evidence against Preece was the statement he had made in Bandon Garda station. Counsel for the defence said that someone convicted on that statement might not feel they had got justice in an Irish court.

As both sides settled down to wait for the jury to decide on the fate of the three accused men, few could have imagined that yet another hurdle would be placed in the way of a conclusion. However, the trial, which had involved more than sixty witnesses, sensationally came to an end, less than an hour into the jury's deliberations. The problem occurred when one of the jurors spotted that they had been given a statement that contained information which had not been put to them in evidence during the trial. Defence legal representatives applied for the jury to be discharged. Patrick McCarthy SC said the Court of Criminal Appeal had quashed a conviction in a case where a similar error had occurred. For the prosecution, Donal McCarthy said it was a matter for the trial judge to decide whether or not the jury should proceed with their deliberations.

A reluctant Judge AG Murphy said he did not have a choice in the matter and conceded that the jury should be discharged. According to the *Irish Examiner,* he said: 'An irregularity has been brought to our attention which is an irregularity of a character which makes it impossible for you to continue your deliberations. Mistakes happen and there we are – you are discharged. You do not have to come back again.'

By now, prosecution of the three men had turned into a farcical situation. A new trial was scheduled to get underway on 2 May, with a new jury who would hear the evidence again. Preece, Court and Simpkins were once again remanded in custody, ahead of the new trial. However, the end of the road had come in their big fight against the prosecution. A day after the collapse of the trial, they landed a huge surprise on all who had been fascinated by the *Posidonia* saga. They all pleaded guilty to the charge of having more than £10,000 worth of cannabis resin for sale or supply, and the importation charge was dropped. The development meant that the men could now be sentenced. For Simpkins, the outcome meant that he was now certain of facing several years away from his young child. Just before the sentencing, a photograph of his child was given to Judge Murphy to highlight this.

When sentencing the men, Judge Murphy made a clear distinction between Preece and his two colleagues. He said that the skipper was the most culpable of the trio and had enlisted Court and Simpkins in the operation. Preece was given a nine-year sentence, while his colleagues were each sentenced to eight years in prison. The sentences were backdated to 16 November 1999 and Preece's was due to expire in November 2008. His accomplices were released a year earlier. Court and Simpkins were repatriated to serve the remainder of their sentences in the UK in 2002, while Preece was repatriated in 2003.

In handing down the sentences, Judge Murphy defended his decision not to give the men the mandatory ten-year sentence for the offence. He said the men had given assistance to investigating officers on the case and that the men's decision to plead guilty to one charge had saved the State the cost of a third trial. He added: 'These men could be said to be not normally bad men, not professional criminals. They are ordinary men who were strapped for money and lured into this by those who are more seriously involved. They foolishly and wrongly fell for the lure of the easy money and agreed to act as couriers of these drugs.' He told the court that he was very aware of the damage caused by drugs to weak and foolish people who use them, and of the gross culpability of the people who supply and assist in supplying them.

As the saga came to an end, Judge Murphy ordered that the cannabis found on board the *Posidonia* be destroyed. As is typical with any seizure involving a vessel, Judge Murphy also directed that the converted trawler be confiscated by the State. The usual step of selling the boat was not taken by the Revenue Commissioners on this occasion, however. Instead, the boat was donated to the St Mary's Maritime Project in Limerick, a city plagued by drug-related crime. A proposal was submitted by the group to restore the damaged boat. The work was to be carried out by a team of young people, who were either at risk or had left school early. The vessel was then to be deployed for leisure and corporate use and crewed by some of the people involved in the restoration project.

Once the successful bid was made, the *Posidonia* was towed to the Shannon Foynes Harbour Company's docks from

Kinsale. The *Posidonia* was later moved to a site belonging to Limerick City Council, in the Corcanree Industrial Estate, off the Dock Road. Premises were made available to the group for the refurbishment of the vessel. Refurbishment is likely to take two years and was due to get underway in 2008.

Financial backing of £12,500 for the towing operation was provided by the JP McManus Charitable Foundation. The project later received €150,000 from the Dormant Accounts Fund.

Chapter 11

DUNLOUGH BAY

As the man reached shore from the unforgiving waters of Dunlough Bay, he knew he had to get help. He could see his colleague still in the water and there was no hope of him being able to swim to safety. Panicked, the young man grabbed on to his holdall and looked around for someone to raise the alarm. However, it was not yet 7.00am and there was nobody to be seen in the rocky inlet.

It was 2 July 2007 and the Englishman had been overthrown from a rib in the seas off Mizen Head, in West Cork. Saturated wet, he decided to go to one of the houses he could see in the distance. Knocking on the door of one of the farmhouses, he hoped someone would hear him. Although it was still early, his knock was answered.

When Michael O'Donovan opened his farmhouse door, he was confronted by a stranger, who was shivering and soaking wet. The shaken young man explained that he had been out fishing with two friends and that their rib had been overturned by the rough seas. He said he was originally from

Monaghan, his name was Gerard O'Leary and that, ironically, that day was his birthday. According to O'Leary, one of his friends was still in the rough waters lashing off the rocks of Dunlough Bay but he stressed a number of times that there was no need to call the emergency services. Michael O'Donovan gave the visitor a hot drink and a change of clothes. Although it was July, Ireland had been experiencing a particularly bad summer and the sea conditions in recent days had been similar to wintry storms. As a result, O'Leary's tale came as little surprise.

Despite his protestations that his friends would be safe, Michael O'Donovan decided to look out to sea himself to check on them. He saw a small watercraft sailing around a headland towards Mizen Head, with what appeared to be just one crew member on board. Still worried about the possibility of someone being in trouble in the sea, he decided something had to be done and he contacted his sister, who in turn raised the alarm. As Gerard O'Leary was being looked after, a call was put in with the coastguard about the overturned rib and the possibility of his friend being lost at sea. Members of the local coastguard team arrived, shortly afterwards, and the young man told them he had been staying with friends locally in recent days.

There was a strong possibility that Gerard O'Leary could suffer hypothermia and efforts were made to warm him up to prevent this happening. Meanwhile, members of the coast-guard made their way to the nearby pier to launch a search and rescue operation for O'Leary's friend. When they got there, a green British-registered jeep was parked in front, and two men were standing nearby. Both were strangers and did not arouse suspicion, at first, as the coastguard's priority was locating the man in the sea. Indeed, by now there was also talk of another man being in the water, and emergency volunteers were busy with the rescue operation.

A man could be seen in the water, and it was clear he was wearing a life jacket. With such rough seas, there was nothing left to chance – a major rescue operation was launched. Now that the coastguard members knew he was wearing a life jacket, they were hopeful of a safe recovery. A lifeboat from Castletownbere had been alerted to come to the scene, and was on its way. Its crew were surprised at the early call out on a Monday morning. However, they were regularly called out to help in similar incidents, and headed towards Dunlough Bay, arriving there shortly after 9.00am. A rescue helicopter was also enlisted in the operation.

Space was at a premium on the tiny roadway leading down to the bay. Without thinking, a member of the coastguard parked his vehicle in front of the green jeep. The move effec-tively blocked the path of the vehicle. Others began to arrive at the scene shortly afterwards, including Gardaí who had also been contacted about the emergency. Further vehicles were also parked in the way of the jeep. Emergency workers got their operation underway, giving little thought at first to the two strangers. Indeed, as far as they were aware, the priorities of the two men seen near the jeep were also focused on saving the men, particularly as one of the strangers told the emergency workers there was a man in the water who needed saving.

However, the increasing presence of Gardaí, and other emergency workers at the scene, had taken the concentration off the two strangers long enough for them to disappear from the scene. They opted to leave their jeep blocked by the rescue vehicles, while they escaped through the fields. While the emergency volunteers had rushed to the scene, the man known as Gerard O'Leary had remained in a distressed condition in the nearby house. He was taken away to Bantry General Hospital, shortly afterwards, by one of two ambulances that had arrived at the scene. Despite the efforts of locals, it was suspected he had developed hypothermia as a result of his ordeal.

Emergency personnel felt it was important to get as many details as possible about the circumstances of the men's arrival into Dunlough Bay, as they prepared for the rescue of one of O'Leary's friends and the search for the other one. However, they began to feel that the young man who had raised the alarm was being slightly evasive with some answers. When they reached the pier, they quickly began to piece together the answers themselves. Several large packets could be seen floating in the sea near the overturned rib and the man they were trying to save. When the lifeboat crew arrived from Castletownbere, they quickly pulled the man from the cold sea, and the coastguard helicopter airlifted him to shore. It was evident that he too was suffering from hypothermia, and he was wrapped in blankets before being laid onto a stretcher. He was given oxygen at the scene, before being removed by ambulance to the nearest hospital, in Bantry.

While he was being treated at the scene, he managed to urge the lifeboat crew to keep searching – as there had been three of them out on the rib. He also told them that his own name was Anthony. Although there was an urgency among emergency workers to continue their search for the third man, their attentions were also taken up by the packets in the sea. Up to fifty mysterious packages could be seen and Gardaí believed they had inadvertently come across a drug smuggling operation that had fallen foul of the weather. It was time to extend the operation from a rescue mission to a drug investigation, while rescue teams continued their search for another man.

Members of the West Cork drugs unit arrived at the scene, from Bandon, after 11.00am that morning, joined by members of the customs drug enforcement team on board the service's only boat, *An Suirbhéir*. The *LE Orla* was also dispatched to the scene as part of the inter-agency taskforce approach to the operation. As the bales were winched from the water by the helicopter, the search continued for a further two hours for the alleged missing third man. However, after 1.00pm, a decision was taken to step down the search, as it became obvious that there was nobody else in the water. It was becoming increasingly unlikely that the men, now being treated in hospital, had been on a fishing trip, as Gerard O'Leary had claimed.

By now, some of the bales had been airlifted to shore, and one had been taken to nearby Schull for testing to establish its contents. A preliminary examination of the bale proved the suspicions of Gardaí, customs and the navy – it contained cocaine. This proof gave a new urgency to the recovery mission and the need to interview the two men in hospital. The irony of the seizure was that it came just weeks after a meeting was held in Bandon between law enforcement agencies and maritime residents as part of the Coastal Watch initiative, aimed at reminding people living on the coast to be on the lookout for suspicious activities at sea. There had not been a major shipment apprehended off the coast of Ireland since the seizure of cannabis resin on board the *Posidonia*, near the Fastnet in 1999. It was clear now that the emergency services had stumbled on another major catch off the West Cork coast and the concern was that the shipment could have escaped the authorities, if the seas had not been so rough in Dunlough Bay that morning. However, the fact that someone had put the wrong fuel in the rib's engine was another key factor. Quoted in the *Evening Echo*, senior counsel Blaise O'Carroll, later said: 'Some idiot put diesel into it when he should have put petrol in it and the engine lost its power and ended up on rocks.'

Gardaí were at the hospital after 2.00pm that afternoon, when O'Leary was discharged. Confident now that the rib's accident at sea had led them to a major drug smuggling effort, the officers arrested O'Leary and took him to the nearby Garda station for questioning under drug trafficking legislation. Meanwhile, a major land search was underway on Mizen Head to trace the two men who had left the scene at Dunlough Bay. Investigators were convinced of a connection between them, the men in the hospital and the cocaine bales. They had managed to draw suspicion on themselves by telling the rescue workers to help the man in the sea, but failing to stay in the area to see if they could assist in the operation.

The crew of the Baltimore lifeboat had also been drafted in by now. The bales of cocaine were airlifted onto the lifeboat. For the Baltimore crew, the operation was not like anything they had ever been tasked to do before. However, they took to their new role easily and loaded more than fifty bales onto the lifeboat. The cargo was removed to Baltimore where the bales were then taken into the possession of customs by Paddy O'Sullivan, before being transferred to Bantry Garda station. An incident room had been set up at the station, under the direction of Detective Chief Superintendent Tony Quilter, and 150 Gardaí were assigned to the different strands of the investigation. As the operation had developed, personnel had been drafted in from Cork city and national units including the Garda National Drugs Unit, the National Bureau of Criminal Investigation, the Air Support Unit and the Technical Bureau.

As officers combined all elements of the investigation, one man living on the nearby Sheep's Head peninsula grew increasingly worried for his son's safety. Joe Daly Senior had heard radio news reports about the massive rescue operation off Mizen Head and feared his son had been lost at sea. He had been living in the area, after moving from England, in recent years. His sons were in the area on holidays for a couple of weeks. He had come to his house that morning to borrow a rib to go fishing, and he had not heard from them since. Other members of his family contacted Gardaí and the worried man was taken to Bantry to visit the two men in hospital. Neither was his son Joe. However, he instantly recognised the man who had been plucked from the sea and said he was one of his sons' friends. He told Gardaí the man's name was Martin. Unwittingly, the man further raised the suspicions of officers about what the men had been doing when the accident happened. Mr Daly's assertion that the man was named Martin was a contradiction of what the rescued man had already told them. Subsequent investigations revealed his name was actually Martin Wanden, a UK national from Kent. Wanden had no fixed address but had a home in South Africa.

The day turned into night and Joe Daly still had not returned to his father's house. The two men who had been seen at Dunlough Bay had still not been traced either and checkpoints were mounted on the peninsula, in an effort to find them. If the men had been in the area for genuine purposes, why had they disappeared when they knew at least one man was fighting for his life in the water? Investigators keen to find an answer to that question had alerted locals to be on the lookout for the two men. Gardaí on foot and in patrol cars searched for the men on the ground, while a helicopter also flew over the surrounding areas to determine where the men were. With a tight security ring around the area, it was felt they could not have gone far, especially as their jeep was left behind at Dunlough Bay. Over the next twenty-four hours, reports of two dishevelled men being seen between the bay and Schull were made to Gardaí, but they still managed to evade the authorities.

The investigation now had many strands, including regular

checks with hospital staff in Bantry to check on the condition of the man who had been plucked from the sea. In the nearby Garda station, the young man who had raised the alarm was now being questioned about a possible link to a drug smuggling enterprise. It was becoming clear that the botched effort would have been the largest ever consignment of cocaine to have been brought into Ireland, if the weather had not been so stormy. Sixty-one bales of the Class A drug were recovered from the sea over the two days following the rescue operation, and Gardaí estimated the haul was worth a staggering €107 million. A further one was recovered months later – on 27 November, when all hope had been given up of retrieving it. Like the rest of the bales, it weighed 25kg and was worth a €1.75 million – a figure which would have made it a very significant seizure, if found on its own in any other drug enforcement operation on land. The provisional value was reached on the basis that the cocaine had a purity of between 12 per cent to 15 per cent. However, analysis of the haul revealed it had a purity of 75 per cent – bringing the street value to a massive €440 million, as it was likely it would have been mixed with an agent to make it go further, if it had not been seized. One of those giving evidence was forensic expert Geraldine O'Neill, who said recent tests of cocaine sold in Ireland showed that the average purity of cocaine in early 2008 was 6.7 per cent. If broken down to this level, the Dunlough Bay seizure could have an estimated value of €1.2 billion.

Other items had also been taken from the water in the immediate aftermath of the seizure. These included the rib, debris and a global positioning system – which would later prove vital in the investigation. A waterproof box was also taken from the water and it held a satellite phone, which was undamaged by its time in the sea. Each item was carefully removed to preserve all vital evidence, before being sent for technical analysis.

As Wanden remained in a stable condition for two days after the rescue operation, Gardaí continued their search for the two men who had left the scene. Literally forty-eight hours after Wanden had been taken from the sea, officers received vital information from a man living on the Mizen peninsula. He had seen two men walking along a roadway several kilometres from Dunlough Bay, at a place called Gubbeen, Schull. He believed they were the men Gardaí had been looking for. Local Sergeant Gerard Prenderville followed up the information and met the two men walking along the road. When he questioned them, they gave very little information. They were both arrested and taken to Bantry Garda Station. The two men cut dishevelled figures but were in good condition, despite being at the mercy of the elements for two nights without food or beds. Their arrests were a mixed blessing for the Daly family as one of them was the missing Joe Daly. The

Right: Christopher 'Golly' O'Connell, convicted for smuggling drugs on the *Karma of the East*. (Courtesy of the *Evening Echo/Irish Examiner*.)

Below: The *Plongeur Wisky* in Kilrush. (Courtesy of Paddy O'Sullivan.)

Above: The *Plongeur Wisky* docked in Kilrush. (Courtesy of Paddy O'Sullivan.)

Right: Kevin Lafferty, skipper of the *Plongeur Wisky*. (Courtesy of the *Evening Echo/Irish Examiner*.)

Above: Gardaí on duty in Goleen, Dunlough Bay case.

Below: A naval diver searching under the *Tia*. Ultimately no drugs were found on the *Tia*. (Courtesy of the *Evening Echo/Irish Examiner*.)

Left: Chief Supt. Kevin Ludlow, Dunlough Bay case.

Right: Dr Chris Luke, emergency consultant. (Courtesy of the *Evening Echo/Irish Examiner*.)

Right: Gerard Hagan, of the
Dunlough Bay case.
(Courtesy of Richard
Mills/*Evening Echo*.)

Below: Perry Wharrie, of the Dunlough Bay case. (Courtesy of *Evening
Echo/Irish Examiner*.)

Above: Emergency operation in Dunlough Bay. (Courtesy of Richard Mills/*Evening Echo*.)

Below: Drugs floating in Dunlough Bay. (Courtesy of Richard Mills/*Evening Echo*.)

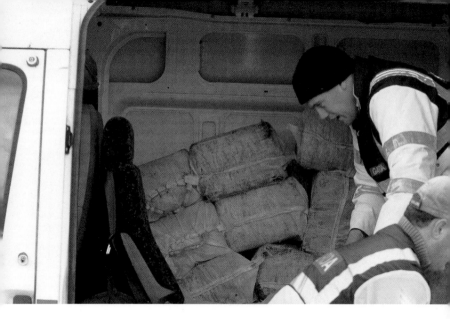

Above: Gardaí loading bales of cocaine into a van after they were rescued from Dunlough Bay. (Courtesy of Richard Mills/*Evening Echo*.)

Below: Martin Wanden lies on a stretcher, after being taken from the waters of Dunlough Bay. (Courtesy of Richard Mills/*Evening Echo*.)

Above: Gardaí in Crookhaven during the investigation into the Dunlough Bay seizure. (Courtesy of Richard Mills/*Evening Echo*.)

Below: The home of Martin Wanden in Cape Town. (Courtesy of Asset Forfeiture Unit, South Africa.)

other man was identified as Englishman Perry Wharrie from Pryles Lane, Loughton, Essex, who had also been staying locally in recent weeks. The two were later removed to Bandon Garda station to enable the recording of their interviews, as there were not enough facilities in Bantry to deal with all the prisoners.

Case officers knew there was a substantial network of people behind the consignment lost to the rough sea. The green jeep parked near Dunlough Bay was seized as evidence, and investigations led customs officers and Gardaí to two other jeeps parked in the nearby village of Crookhaven, also on the Mizen peninsula. The vehicles were removed from the tourist village for technical examinations to help establish vital missing links in the investigation. Joe Daly had links to the adjoining Sheep's Head peninsula, through his father, and it was only a matter of time before officers widened their net to cover that area as well. A suspect Volkswagen Passat was found on that peninsula, in the village of Ahakista. It was also discovered that two houses, a short distance away in Kilcrohane, had been rented in recent weeks by the three of the four men and a number of others who were suspected of having been the landing party for the drugs. Another rib had also been found in Durrus, the village where the two peninsulas met. That rib was taken away for examination as well. It was suspected that it had been intended to use the vessel to transfer drugs. It was now clear that the arrival of the drugs into Dunlough Bay was a major mistake caused by the chaotic seas. It was far more likely that an inlet on the Sheep's Head peninsula had been the intended landing point.

The discovery of the Volkswagen Passat in Ahakista was a vital stroke for the investigation team. Three mobile phones were seized from the car. Gardaí hoped that analysis of communication traffic involving the phones could provide valuable information. Most significant, however, was a key document involving the young man who had raised the alarm after the rib overturned. Until now, he was believed to be named O'Leary and have strong links to Monaghan. However, when his genuine passport was discovered in the Passat, it quickly emerged that the O'Leary passport was false and that his real name was Gerard Hagan. Armed with this information, officers took the twenty-three-year-old to Macroom District Court to have his period of detention extended by Judge James McNulty, under the provisions of drug trafficking legislation. With court extensions, he could be held for up to seven days and officers felt the investigation was so expansive that they required the extra time to help build a case. It emerged in court evidence from Chief Superintendent Kevin Ludlow that Hagan had obtained the false passport in the name of a dead baby from Monaghan, whose birthday was, ironically, the date of the Dunlough Bay seizure. Hagan's own birthday was in April, and he was from Hollowcroft in Liverpool. The application for the passport had been made through the name of a firm of solicitors allegedly based in London. However, the firm did not exist.

The O'Leary passport helped officers establish the route used by the group behind the operation. It had been stamped in a Caribbean port with the name *Lucky Day* and this gave investigators the clue they were looking for in helping them track the mother ship from which the cocaine had been transferred to the smaller rib. Officers established that the *Lucky Day* catamaran had travelled from the island of Margarita through the Caribbean, with stop-offs in Trinidad and Tobago, and Barbados. It progressed from there at the end of May, arriving at a point off the Mizen Head over a month later. It was believed the transfer of drugs took place at that point over a number of hours early on 2 July.

The false passport revealed Hagan had travelled to Trinidad and Tobago on 19 April 2007, and arrived in Barbados on 6 May on board the *Lucky Day*. The vessel was checked by local law enforcement officers on 19 April and there were three people on it – two Lithuanians and a man who gave his name as Gerard O'Leary. He produced a passport in that name and was the man now known to be Hagan.

The passport was not the only thing to prove a connection to the *Lucky Day*. Communication between two satellite phones – one of which was in the waterproof box – also helped establish a link. Phone records of the phone found in Dunlough Bay revealed a number of calls between it and another satellite phone, which was later established to have been on the *Lucky Day*. Satellite phone technology allows for the identification of locations where the phone is when calls are received or made, through global positioning system technology. As a result, analysis of the calls made to and from the satellite phone on the *Lucky Day* enabled Commander Eugene Ryan, of the naval service, to plot charts showing the catamaran's progress across the Caribbean and the Atlantic, before its arrival off Mizen Head.

The catamaran had been bought just months previously, after it had been advertised for sale on an internet website. The ten-year-old vessel had been built by French company Fontaine Pajot and was advertised at a price of $132,000. The boat was brought from Florida in March for the venture, which ended up in the seizure of the cocaine in Dunlough Bay.

Officers guessed the *Lucky Day* was at sea, moving further and further away from the south coast of Ireland after its long journey. Frantic efforts were being made to trace it by one team of officers, while another team were trying to locate at least six men believed to have been part of the landing party for the drugs in West Cork. Following the seizure in

Dunlough Bay, the men had disappeared. Their disappearance was noted by locals, who had come to know the men in recent weeks as they had mingled among residents in bars, hotels and shops. Some had even played golf on golf courses around West Cork. In the weeks leading up to the seizure, men had stayed in local bed and breakfast establishments and hotels, giving addresses from various parts of England, including Kent. CCTV footage from businesses were scrutinised and the focus had been extended to include footage from airports and ports across Ireland to determine if, how and when they had left the country.

On the troubled seas, the navy and customs officers were still looking for floating bales of cocaine, with searches being conducted from first light. A naval diving team were on standby throughout the week, waiting for an opportunity to search caves in the area for any missing bales.

Back in Bantry town, Gardaí were anxiously awaiting news from hospital staff on Wanden's condition. He was eventually discharged from hospital, three days after he was winched from the sea. Like Hagan, he was arrested immediately and taken for questioning. As his time in custody began, officers prepared to make an application to extend the questioning period for Wharrie and Daly.

The men were brought before Judge McNulty at a special sitting of Clonakilty District Court, amid delight by case officers at news just breaking from Spain that the *Lucky Day* had been successfully traced. While the four men sat in Garda interview rooms in West Cork, two Lithuanians had been making their way steadily towards the Spanish coast on board the catamaran. The boat was detained at sea by Spanish authorities and was brought under escort into the port of La Coruna. It was flying the American flag at the time of its detention. The breakthrough came after Gardaí had enlisted the help of Spanish police, through Interpol, in an effort to trace the mother ship. When the vessel arrived into La Coruna, the two men were taken from the catamaran. Images of them being escorted from the vessel in handcuffs, t-shirts and shorts were broadcast on international television. In Ireland, officers on the case hoped that the capture of the vessel would provide them with evidence which could move the investigation forward. However, there was no trace of any contraband on the *Lucky Day*. The Lithuanian crew members remained in custody for many weeks, but were subsequently released without charge.

In Ireland, another avenue of investigation was the background of the rib found in Dunlough Bay. Enquiries led Gardaí to South Africa. It was established that the vessel had been bought from a company there before being transported to Ireland, through the UK.

Although officers were making advances, they were not

being aided by the four men in custody. Five days on from the seizure, another application was made to extend the detention periods of Wharrie and Daly. A similar application was made for Wanden, who had no fixed address but who had been living in Hout Bay in South Africa until recently. It emerged in court that he was also known as Anthony Claude Lyndon. By now it was felt that there was sufficient evidence against Hagan to charge him. He was taken before Clonakilty District Court on two charges of possessing a controlled substance. One was the more serious charge of having a controlled substance for sale or supply. He was granted free legal aid and remanded in custody.

As he was being escorted to prison, the other three men were still being questioned. A decision was taken to charge Wanden and Daly with similar offences three days later, on 10 July. The men were taken to Skibbereen District Court, arriving amid the scream of sirens, as up to twenty Gardaí surrounded the courthouse. Among the officers were members of the armed Emergency Response Unit. There was little doubt that the botched importation had hit the profits of the network of organisers – and the State was not going to take any chances in relation to security. Both men were also remanded in custody at the hearing and were taken to join Hagan in Cork Prison.

Wharrie was the last to be charged and was brought to

Dunmanway courthouse under tight security the following morning. The intense security visible in Skibbereen the previous day was repeated in Dunmanway. At one point, windows of the tiny courtroom were closed to ensure maximum security. Wharrie was joined at the short hearing by Hagan, who was facing a further remand application by the State. Both were rushed to Cork Prison after the hearing. Officers returned to the incident room in Bantry to work on the preparation of the Book of Evidence.

At this stage, the tentacles of the investigation were spreading all over the world. They extended to Britain, Spain, Eastern Europe, as well as the Caribbean and South America. A clearer picture was beginning to emerge of the men in custody and the major operators pulling the strings in the background. It was clear that the gang were not small-time operators, particularly given the pedigree of the arrested men.

Wharrie was just a month away from his forty-eighth birthday when he was arrested near Schull. He was a married man, who had served a prison sentence for the murder of an English policeman called Frank Mason during an armed robbery of a security van in England. The incident took place outside a bank in Hertfordshire in 1988. He was sentenced to life in prison after being found guilty of PC Mason's murder and charges relating to the possession of a firearm, at Southwark Crown Court in April 1989. Six years later, he was granted conditional release. Among the terms of his release was that he would be under the supervision of the probation service. He was also restricted from travelling or working outside the UK. The released was revoked in January 2006 after he breached the terms, and he was recalled to prison. However, he did not return and was at large until he was arrested in West Cork in 2007. Ironically, another man convicted of murder and firearms offences, following the murder of PC Mason, was caught after being on the run for thirteen years, while Wharrie was in prison awaiting trial in Ireland in November 2007. James Hurley had topped the list of Britain's most wanted criminals and was arrested in the Netherlands. Police in the UK had offered a stg£30,000 award for information on his whereabouts.

Wanden also had a criminal record in Britain, as well as in France. He had no fixed address in England but had known links to Kent where he had married his wife Sonya in 1995. The forty-four-year-old had been linked to drug trafficking operations before the Dunlough Bay seizure, and had convictions in France for possessing and transporting cocaine. At the time of his arrest in West Cork, a European Arrest Warrant was in existence for him. It had been issued in May 2005 by the French authorities, after he had escaped from custody in October 2001. He was wanted for drug trafficking, smuggling of prohibited goods and escaping with the use of violence.

Joe Daly also had convictions. The married father-of-three had been fined in 1990 for assault of a police officer and was given community service in 1998 from Bexley Magistrates Court for possessing an article with a blade or a point in a public place.

Investigations into establishing the key figures behind the scenes revealed that the operation was the culmination of efforts between a number of gangs in the UK, who had forged links with the Medellin cartels in Colombia. Two of the gangs were based in Liverpool, although key figures were by then living in Spain. A gang based in Kent were responsible for organising the logistics of the operation, including key figures who had moved to the south of Ireland for the weeks leading up to the botched effort. While the Book of Evidence was being prepared for the trials of Wanden, Daly, Wharrie and Hagan, efforts were still underway to trace those who had fled from West Cork in the immediate aftermath of the Dunlough Bay seizure.

More than six weeks after the men had been charged, the DPP directed that a further charge – possession of more than €13,000 of a controlled substance for sale or supply – be brought against the four men. That charge carried a mandatory minimum sentence of ten years. By now, the men had been moved to Cloverhill Prison in Dublin for security reasons. The positive aspect of this move was the location of a courthouse adjacent to the prison. This made it easier than the situation in Cork, where large numbers of Gardaí had to travel with the accused from the prison in Cork to courthouses in West Cork because of security concerns.

When the new charges were brought against the men, criticism against the State's decision was voiced by Judge David Anderson at Cloverhill District Court. Under the guidelines governing the DPP, the Book of Evidence is to be served on an accused person within forty-two-days. However, the new charges against the Dunlough Bay four were brought after the forty-two-day period had expired. The judge accused the DPP of buying time over and above what the State allowed, and referred to the move as 'subterfuge'. However, counsel for the State pointed out that investigations were continuing and that the latest charge could only be brought after a detailed forensic examination of the evidence. Despite fears that the men could be released because of the move, they were eventually remanded in continuing custody.

The men were sent forward for trial at Cork Circuit Criminal Court. At a hearing of that court on 11 December, State counsel Tom Creed said that up to 400 witnesses could be called in the men's trial. Mr Creed outlined that the State had already provided 383 witness statements from the Book of Evidence to the men's defence teams. He said a further thirty statements from witnesses, outside the jurisdiction, would also be handed over. The trial got underway on 21 May, under tight security at the courthouse on Cork's Washington Street. On the opening day, selecting a jury to hear the trial proved difficult as many of the panel had holidays booked. Eventually, nine men and three women were sworn in to hear the trial, which was presided over by Judge Seán Ó Donnabháin. The judge said the trial would last up to ten weeks. As expected, legal argument dominated the trial. Hagan had pleaded guilty before the selection of the jury, leaving them to decide on the fates of Wanden, Wharrie and Daly.

Over the course of the trial, witnesses were drawn from the Gardai, customs and navy, as well as locals who had been involved in the rescue operation. Witnesses were also flown in from Barbados, South Africa and Spain to give evidence about the international investigation.

It emerged that Joe Daly's brother, Michael, was by then in custody in the UK, following a significant coastal drugs seizure there. It was reavealed that Michael was a retired detective sergeant in the London Metropolitan Police.

As the jury listened intently to the evidence, they were unaware of two major events which had recently taken place in Wanden's life. His wife Sonya had died some months before the trial got underway and property belonging to the couple in South Africa had been confiscated by the South African Asset Forfeiture Unit.

The property was to be auctioned in South Africa on 8 August, just weeks after the end of the trial. Despite efforts by Wanden and Daly to persuade the jury of their innocence by giving evidence themselves, three unanimous guilty verdicts were delivered in Courtroom number two of Cork Courthouse on 22 July 2008. The jury had taken more than seven hours to decide on the men's fates. A day later, Judge Ó Donnabháin made legal history when he handed down thirty-year sentences to Wanden and Wharrie, along with a twenty-five-year sentence to Daly. Hagan's sentencing was to be held later that year. Addressing the court at the July sentencing hearing, the judge said: 'I think these three defendants are committed and dedicated to this criminal activity. Let's face it, they are in it for the money. They are prepared to deal in drugs, to deal in death and destruction for profit. Let's strip away everything else, that is what they were in it for.' As the three were led away to begin their sentences, fascinated members of the public were in awe. The sentences handed down were the longest ever delivered by a judge in an Irish court for drug offences.

Chapter 12

WANDEN

In the exclusive suburb of Hout Bay in Cape Town, life went on as normal. Unbeknownst to the residents, one of their neighbours had been arrested as part of the probe into Ireland's largest ever seizure of cocaine. However, Martin Wanden's wife, Sonya, found it difficult to go on as normal. Before 2 July 2007, the couple had a lot to look forward to in their adopted home. Now, she was faced with questions about her husband's whereabouts from neighbours. More importantly, her comfortable life was being probed by police.

The recovery of the rib from the waters of Dunlough Bay was a vital part of the jigsaw for investigators in Ireland. Extensive viewing of CCTV led them to believe that the rib had been brought to Ireland from the UK on board a ferry on 15 June – two weeks before the Dunlough Bay seizure. An identification plate with the name of the South African manufacturer was found on the rib after the massive seizure. Documentation found in accommodation used by the men in West Cork also helped to lead officers to a company based in Epping in South Africa, called Boating Dynamix. Tickets found in a jeep seized in the days after the cocaine seizure had revealed that a man using the name Anthony Claude Lyndon had travelled on the same ferry. When investigations broadened to include South Africa, it emerged that a man of that name had regularly travelled there on temporary residence permits and was believed to be Martin Wanden, travelling under an assumed name.

The connection between Wanden and the rib was deemed an integral part of the prosecution's case against him in the Irish investigation. He had claimed he had been on a small red punt which sank after colliding with a bigger vessel. In essence, he had tried to rule out any link to the rib found near the cocaine, despite his proximity to the vessel when he was rescued from Dunlough Bay. However, Wanden's fingerprints were later found on seating and a plastic manifold which had been removed from the rib before the Dunlough Bay incident. These items were recovered during searches of one of the accommodations rented in West Cork by the men suspected of involvement in the cocaine seizure.

Because of the interest in the connection between Wanden and the rib, investigators felt it was necessary to delve into the history of the vessel's origins. Their inquiries in turn led them to their counterparts in South Africa, who helped them paint a picture of Wanden's exclusive lifestyle in Cape Town.

Four weeks after the West Cork seizure, the Chief Officer

of the CAB sent a report to the Asset Forfeiture Unit in South Africa, outlining the circumstances of the Dunlough Bay seizure. Attached to the report was the invoice for the Ballistic 780 rib which had been found near the cocaine. In his report, Detective Chief Superintendent John O'Mahoney listed a number of key questions which Irish authorities sought help in answering. The first was to determine if Wanden had ever visited South Africa. Investigators had a firm belief at this stage that he had links to the country but wanted proof. They were hoping their African counterparts could provide this. The remainder of Detective Chief Superintendent O'Mahoney's requests focused on whether Wanden had purchased the Ballistic 780 rib from Boating Dynamix in Epping, and on how any such transaction and payment were carried out. In his role of CAB Chief Officer, he also wanted to establish if Wanden owned any property in South Africa.

Martin Wanden and his wife Sonya had led a blameless life in South Africa and had not come to the attention of police in their adopted homeland. When inquiries were carried out by the Asset Forfeiture Unit, investigators discovered from the Department of Home Affairs that Wanden had travelled to and from South Africa on numerous occasions, prior to his arrest in West Cork in 2007. At first glance, his most recent visit appeared to have been a week spent there in September 2005. However, closer investigation showed that a man called

Anthony Claude Lyndon, the pseudonym used by Wanden, had also travelled to South Africa between 14 October 2006 and 6 January 2007, and again for two months between 17 March and 17 May 2007. For all these visits, temporary residence permits were issued.

During the second 2007 visit, the Wandens were in the process of finalising the sale of their home at Unit 1 in the La Mer development in Hout Bay. The couple had purchased the property in the Northshore area of Hout Bay in March 2001 and it was registered in Martin Wanden's name on 20 February 2002. The property was purchased at a cost of R1 250 000, with R700 000 of a bond from Nedbank Ltd. On 7 May 2007, the property was sold for R400 000-00 (€32,081.72). At that point, the *Lucky Day* catamaran had just arrived in Barbados, ahead of its journey towards Mizen Head and the arrests there which would see Wanden end up awaiting trial in an Irish prison.

By then, the couple had a new dream home in nearby Llandudno, also in the Hout Bay area. They had purchased the house on 30 March 2003 – a year after the La Mer deal. The property was bought for R4 050 000,00, with the total cost of the transfer costing R4 421 155,00. As far as their new neighbours in Cape Town could see, the Wandens were a very successful couple who now owned two houses in their adopted city. In a sworn affidavit, Asset Forfeiture Unit senior special investigator Johann Joubert said: 'A covering mortgage bond of R2 million was registered against the property in favour of Nedbank Limited on 1 July, 2003. The owners took up only R1 500 000 of this amount to pay towards the purchase price of the property and settled the balance of R2 921 155,00 in cash. However the bank approved a further building bond of R3 million.' According to Mr Joubert, monthly payments of R18 450,95 were made into a Nedbank Ltd account from Wanden's cheque account, which in turn was made up of foreign currency deposits made by Wanden.

When signing official documents for the Llandudno property, the couple both had to declare their occupations. On his form, Wanden informed the lending bank that he was a self-employed building contractor, in keeping with what he had told his new neighbours. His wife also declared herself self-employed but did not elaborate further about her occupation.

Their first home in the La Mer development helped Martin Wanden meet a man involved in selling ribs. After setting up their investigation into Wanden's affairs in South Africa, members of the Asset Forfeiture Unit interviewed the owner of Boating Dynamix. In his statement, he said he first met Martin Wanden in 2004 and that the Briton had bought a 6.5 metre Ballistic rib from him. According to Mr Toerien, payment for the boat was transferred to the company from overseas. The sale went through and two years later, Martin

Wanden approached him again looking for help in finding a larger rib. Boating Dynamix specialised in the sale of such watercraft and Wanden said he wanted a 7.8 metre Ballistic rib for himself and a group of friends in the UK. Mr Toerien advised his customer to approach Boating Dynamix's partner in Hampshire, JBT Marine, who also stocked Ballistic ribs.

According to Toerien's statement: 'Following discussions between Wanden's friends and JBT Marine, they selected a 7.8 metre Ballistic rib fitted with a 250 HP Evinrude Electric Start Engine and a trailer . . . They wanted to pay cash for the boat which JBT Marine could not accept. The boat was then sold back to Boating Dynamix who then sold the boat to Wanden.' Wanden transferred the sum of stg£34,000 into the account of Boating Dynamix on 26 October 2006 and this was then converted into the South African sum of R490 680-00. Mr Toerien added: 'I then arranged with JBT Marine to release the boat to Wanden's friends who took delivery of it. He told me that he wanted the boat to use for pleasure cruises in Europe.' It was this boat that was later found in the waters off the Mizen Head in July 2007.

Mr Toerien and other acquaintances were totally unaware of his background in the UK and Europe. When buying his first home in South Africa, however, he was hiding a dark secret – he was on the run from the French authorities and a European Arrest Warrant had been issued for him. He had

fled from France in 2001, after being arrested by customs officials in Wissant on 4 October of that year. He and an accom-
plice were arrested after the vehicle they were travelling in was
stopped and searched; 84kg of cannabis and 75kg of tobacco
were found in the vehicle. In an interview with French police,
Wanden said he had arrived a day earlier to collect the tobacco
to transport it to the UK and that his local contact was someone named Knuckles. According to his account, the goods
had been loaded onto an inflatable dinghy on Wissant beach
but an attempt to cross the sea with the cargo was abandoned
because of rough seas. It was at this point that a decision was
taken to load the goods into the vehicle in which they were
discovered by customs officials. He gave officers details of at
least two similar attempts that had not succeeded. He also
spoke of a crossing that had gone off without a hitch in the
past, and told them he had been paid a total of €500 for his
involvement.

Two days after his arrest in France, Wanden decided to
escape from the police station in Portel. His bid succeeded at
7.15am that morning. As he fled, he knocked over an officer,
who was minding his cell at the time. Attempts to track down
the Kent man failed. He was sentenced in *abstentia* at a court
sitting in Boulogne Sur Mer in 2003 to two years in prison for
possession and importation of drugs; smuggling banned
goods; smuggling heavily taxed goods, and absconding with

violence. However, Wanden had not re-appeared to serve his sentence. By then, he and his wife were already settling into life in South Africa, and had just signed along the dotted lines to transfer the Llandudno property into their names. The fugitive was regularly travelling to and from South Africa but managed to evade the French authorities.

Evidence of his jet-setting lifestyle was laid out in a document to the South African authorities by Detective Chief Superintendent O'Mahoney of the CAB. The document stated: 'Information received at this office indicates that Martin Wanden was stopped at London Heathrow, Terminal 4, on 27 August, 2005 disembarking from an inbound flight from Cape Town, South Africa. His passport bore immigration stamps from numerous countries, including the USA, Mauritius, Namibia, Zimbabwe and South Africa. Specifically, in the case of South Africa, there were several temporary residence permits.' In an accompanying affidavit, Detective Inspector Sean Healy said: 'I have information that Wanden is well known to the law enforcement agencies in the UK, Netherlands, France, Spain, Portugal and Ireland for the importation of drugs from South America to Europe.' According to an Interpol document, there was intelligence that Wanden had been of interest to the authorities in Britain since 1994, as he was suspected of being involved in the importation of Class B drugs by rib. Intelligence received in 2000 indicated that

Wanden's drugs of choice for importation had since been upgraded to Class A drugs.

When he was stopped at Heathrow airport, it was evident that he knew he was wanted in France. However, the British authorities could not arrest him. At that point, the European Arrest Warrant had not been accepted in the UK, and it did not become valid there until later that year. He was arrested shortly afterwards and granted conditional bail, with an extradition hearing scheduled for 1 March 2006. However, he did not turn up for the hearing and remained at large, until a twist of fate landed him in the seas of Dunlough Bay, sixteen months later.

With his neighbours ignorant of his background, Wanden used the Irish building boom as a perfect cover for his extravagant lifestyle and his regular trips abroad. He wrote on official bank documents that he was a building contractor and told Toerien he was working with a construction company overseas. He was more specific about locations with another man called Vernon Murray, whom he told that he was working in Ireland. Vernon Murray first met Martin Wanden in 2005 through the Atlantic Boat Club in Hout Bay. He regularly met the Wandens at functions at the club and he knew Martin owned a rib, which was stored in the nearby Hout Bay boatyard. Wanden brought vehicles to him for repair at Speedy Tyre and Exhaust company in Paarden Island. In a statement to the South African authorities in October 2007, Mr Murray recalled: 'Martin introduced himself as being from the UK and doing developments in Ireland. He never elaborated more and did not speak about it at all. You had to question him about it if you wanted to know something about his work. He used to travel abroad on a regular base (sic).'

The Wandens' wealth was obvious, even in an area which was frequented by the affluent of South African society. Mr Murray said: 'They seemed to be very wealthy and had no qualms in spending a lot of money. He was the owner of a black Range Rover motor vehicle with registration number WAND1. Sonya used to drive the vehicle as Martin purchased it for her on her birthday.' Legislation in some provinces in South Africa allows vehicle owners to have personalised registration numbers, as in the case of the Wandens. The Range Rover's full registration plate was WAND1WP, with the WP representing the Western Province. This was another indicator of the couple's wealth, as vehicle owners have to pay extra for the privilege of having a personalised registration plate. The cost is dependent on the number of digits or letters included in the registration number.

When digging into Wanden's affairs, the Range Rover had come on the radar of the Asset Forfeiture Unit and led them to the door of Mr Murray. By this stage, Wanden had been arrested in Ireland and was not in a position to return to South

Africa, where Mr Murray was waiting for the Englishman to pay him for repair work done to the Range Rover.

In his statement to investigators, Mr Murray explained: 'Wanden damaged this vehicle at one stage. He bumped the vehicle into something. The bonnet, grill and other sections in the front of the vehicle was damaged. The rims and tyres were also damaged. This happened round about May or June of this year. He requested me to get the vehicle repaired for him as he was on his way abroad again. I often do these type of things for members of the club. He told me that he was going to repay me on his return as we have done this on previous occasions.' Mr Murray agreed and the cost of the work came to R48 500-00.

As time passed on, it became apparent that Wanden was unlikely to return, and Mr Murray became concerned because the bill remained unpaid. He decided to ask Sonya about her husband's whereabouts. She was vague in details of his travel arrangements and Mr Murray felt further investigation was necessary. He trawled through the internet and discovered to his horror that Wanden was in prison in Ireland, accused of involvement in that country's largest ever seizure of cocaine. It was obvious that he was not coming back to South Africa any time soon. Vernon Murray knew it was time to approach Sonya again to discuss payment. Eventually, they came to an agreement about the money owed by Wanden: 'As she could not pay me the money she made a suggestion to me that I accepted. She told me that I could take the rib and sell it. I could then deduct the money owed to me when the boat is sold and give the difference to her.' Mr Murray took the boat, which was the first one Wanden had bought from Boating Dynamix, and he put it up for sale at a price of R120 000-00. However, by the time the investigators arrived at his door in October, the rib had not been sold and they took possession of it as part of their attempts to freeze the Wandens' assets.

With her husband in prison, Sonya had to face the reality that their dream life was nearing an end. Money worries were on her mind, prompting her to also get rid of the Range Rover that her husband had bought for her birthday. When the Asset Forfeiture Unit got their investigation underway into the couple's financial dealings, it emerged that the Range Rover had been given to a man called Robert Pierce of Westcape Construction (Pty) Ltd. Similar to the circumstances of the rib given to Mr Murray, the stricken woman gave Mr Pierce the vehicle as payment for building works he was carrying out on the Llandudno property.

With pressure mounting, Sonya Wanden attempted to take vast funds from the couple's South African accounts. However, by now news was filtering through to Cape Town that Martin Wanden had been linked to the Irish drugs find. When bank officials in Nedbank Ltd became suspicious of transactions being made involving the couple's accounts, they contacted the Financial Intelligence Centre. The centre in turn enlisted the Asset Forfeiture Unit. Investigator Johann Joubert's affidavit revealed that this contact was received on 14 September 2007. The investigator said: 'In terms of the information provided to me by the Centre, Sonja (sic) Wanden was at a Nedbank branch on 12 September 2007 attempting to withdraw large sums of money from Wanden's Nedbank cheque account ... The bank, aware of newspaper reports relating to the arrest of Wanden on drug trafficking charges, contacted the Centre to report its suspicions relating to the funds in the account and to determine whether to proceed with the transaction. Mrs Wanden had written two cheques. One of R50,000.00 was cashed and a further cheque of R350,000.00 was awaiting authorisation.'

An intervention order was issued by the Director of the Financial Intelligence Centre two days later, to prevent further movement on the account. As a result, Nedbank declined to honour the cheque which was awaiting authorisation and the account was frozen, leaving Sonya Wanden with no access to its contents.

Up until now, the activities of the Asset Forfeiture Unit had only been carried out to assist the Irish authorities in their delving into Wanden's affairs. However, a decision was taken to launch an investigation domestically in South Africa by the

Asset Forfeiture Unit, and the aid of the police was called upon. The domestic investigation looked forensically at the Wandens' banking arrangements, under the Prevention of Organised Crime Act 121 of 1998. The investigation was set up to prove Martin Wanden's assets were financed either by the proceeds of crime or the instruments of a crime. Investigators discovered the couple held three accounts with Nedbank Ltd. These included the non-resident cheque account and two bond accounts. The cheque account was opened on 26 March 2001 and the signatories were the Wandens and another woman.

For the purpose of the cheque account, Sonya signed her surname as Negib, her name before she had married Wanden. Money was readily fed into it through regular foreign exchange deposits. The funds were used mainly for bond repayments but were also used for bills including health and insurance payments. It also appeared to investigators that money had been taken from the account to pay for Persian carpets and antiques. A significant lodgement was made on 29 August 2007, as Martin Wanden languished in an Irish prison, awaiting trial. A cheque to the sum of R1 660 493,82 was lodged by Ashersons attorneys and was recorded by Nedbank Ltd as being the proceeds from the sale of property. On 22 October 2007 the balance in the account was R1 537 951,15.

By now, Sonya Wanden felt it was time to make a decision about her future. With her husband in prison in Ireland and the attentions of the police and financial investigators on top of her, she explored the possibility of leaving Cape Town. The exclusive suburb where she had made her home was no longer as welcoming to her. It was time to sell what property the couple had, and leave. The Asset Forfeiture Unit was informed of Sonya's decision to move on 4 October, in a phone call from Antony Arvan of Maurice Phillips Wisenberg Attorneys. Investigator Joubert's statement of events said: 'He advised me that he represents Sonja (sic) Wandon (sic) and that she had instructed him to dispose of all her assets in South Africa as she intended leaving the country. He indicated that he understood that the Asset Forfeiture Unit was conducting investigations into Wandon (sic) and Mrs Wandon's (sic) affairs and wanted to know if I knew of any reason why he could not carry out her instructions.' He gave the confirmation Mr Arvan had asked for, digesting the new information that Mrs Wanden was planning to leave.

There had been no indication given of where the stricken Mrs Wanden was planning to flee for safety. However, on 15 October, the Financial Intelligence Centre informed Mr Joubert that she had requested Nedbank Ltd to transfer any funds in the couple's cheque account to an account in England. Another intervention order was issued to prevent movement on the account. Three days later, Joubert contacted Mr Arvan to establish if court papers for Sonya Wanden would be accepted by him. He said he could not contact her and that she had returned to the UK at that point.

In an affidavit to the High Court in Cape Town, Johann Joubert outlined the entire investigation into the financial affairs of the Wandens. His statement concluded: 'I submit that from the above there are reasonable grounds to believe that the property which forms the subject matter of this application was acquired with the proceeds of Wanden's drug trafficking or constitute property representing such property.'

The views of the investigators were accepted by the Cape High Court, which placed a preservation order on Wanden's properties and bank accounts on 22 October 2007. This allowed the authorities to freeze the couple's assets while they continued their efforts to confiscate them. However, the process hit a stumbling block in March of the following year, when it emerged that Sonya Wanden had killed herself in a British psychiatric hospital, in November 2007. She was cited as an interested party in the proceedings, along with her husband. Also cited were Vernon Murray and Westcape Construction (Pty) Ltd, because they were now in possession of the Range Rover and the rib originally purchased by Martin Wanden.

With his wife dead and himself awaiting trial in Ireland, the future looked bleak for Wanden. However, it was to get worse. Three weeks before his trial kicked off, a decision was taken in the High Court in Cape Town to confiscate his assets. In the order, Mr Justice Cleaver directed that the Llandudno home, his jeep, the rib and a trailer were all to be forfeited. Also included in the order was the money in the Nedbank cheque account. A *curator bonis*, Andre Var Heerden of SAB&T Insolvencies and Corporate Recoveries (Pty) Ltd, was appointed to oversee the sale of the property. Included in the order was a direction that R2 386 474.30, along with interest of 15.5% per annum effective from 20 February 2008, be paid to Maurice Philips Wisenberg Attorneys, who were acting on behalf of construction company Westcape Construction (Pty) Ltd. The order also directed the *curator bonis* to deduct his own fees and disbursements, approved by the High Court. The remainder of the funds raised through the sale of the property were then to be paid into the Criminal Assets Recovery Account.

The property was to be auctioned by the ClareMart Auction Group on 8 August 2008, just two weeks after he achieved notoriety in Ireland for being handed the longest-ever prison sentence for drugs offences in that country.

Chapter 13

EFFECTS ON SOCIETY

Liam tentatively handed over the cannabis to his young clients, secretly terrified he would get caught. The thirteen-year-old dealer was new on the scene and eager to make money from school friends to fund his own drug habit. Liam had been smoking hash for two years now. He also got a buzz from sniffing petrol, like some of his older friends.

When Liam started smoking cannabis, he had no idea how quickly he would become dependant on drugs. Smoking cannabis was just another thing to do with his group of friends. When someone suggested trying cocaine and Ecstasy, there was nothing to lose. Or so he thought. However, snorting his first line, when he was just fourteen-years-old, was the start of a downward spiral into drug addiction, family rejection and a foot on the crime ladder.

Smoking joints had been less of a financial drain than his new habit. Within months, he was in debt to the tune of €5,000 – a sum that had to be paid by his parents when his dealers came knocking on his unsuspecting family's door. When it became clear to his parents that Liam had a drug addiction, they knew they had to look outside the family for help. By now, their son had already been in trouble with the law and was being seen by a Juvenile Liaison Officer. Working together, the officer and his parents sent him to a treatment centre in the hope that he would recover from his addiction. Looking back now, the twenty-one-year-old recovering addict says: 'I wanted to stop but I didn't know the extent of my problem.' As a result, he did not take the residential treatment centre seriously and was thrown out of the six-week programme with just one week remaining. The after-care programme he attended did not benefit him much either – he returned to alcohol and drug use within six months. His penchant for drugs knew few boundaries, although he never used heroin. He returned to cocaine, cannabis and Ecstasy with a vengeance, and also began using prescription drugs like Valium, which he bought on the black market.

The insatiable hunger for the illegal substances meant that Liam was also forced back into dealing. This time, it was a world away from the small time dealing of his early teens and he had a ready market for cocaine and cannabis. As time went on, his client base grew to a couple of hundred clients.

Although a budding success in the drugs trade, his personal life was falling apart. He had dropped out of school and had been thrown out of his family home. Moving in with a friend of his, who was also in the drugs scene, seemed like a logical step. In essence however, it led him further into a black hole of drug use, dealing and crime to fund his habit. He began breaking in to premises to steal money, but he was caught one night in possession of firearms, which he had stolen from a house. Gardaí were called after he fired a shotgun and he was charged in relation to the break-in and using the firearm. Liam faced a five-year sentence – unless he went for treatment again. He returned to the centre he had been thrown out of. At this stage he was more emotionally mature and accepting of his dire circumstances and the extent of his addiction. He decided to give treatment a chance, and had also tried to make amends with his family. Things were looking up for him, when he left the centre, and his family sent him to a boarding school – in the hope that moving away from his old base would help bring him the new start and direction they felt he needed.

Eager to get back to a life where drugs did not control him, Liam went to Alcoholics Anonymous (AA) meetings in the town where he was living and started with Narcotics Anonymous (NA), when he returned home for the summer holidays. The seventeen-year-old felt like a fish out of water among the middle-aged users attending the meetings, but their support made him feel easier in their company within a short space of time. However, the draw to drugs was not easy to ignore and he returned to his old habits after he had completed his

Leaving Certificate exams. The easy money made through drug dealing tempted him back to the trade when he found it difficult to get a full-time job. He managed to deal without using for a short period but very soon was hooked on drugs again. Once more, the despair and disappointment resulted in his family forcing him to leave home and he moved back to the city to live with his girlfriend. Unknown to her, he had become a dealer in a drugs empire, as he needed to have ready cash to pay for his €1,200-per-week cocaine and cannabis habit. He remembers: 'I was about eighteen years old at the time and was involved in a major distribution network in my home city and my life was under threat as a result, because of disputes with other groups about drugs. I was selling from my apartment and also drove around to meet my clients. I had a couple of hundred customers and had people selling stuff for me as well.'

A massive clampdown on organised and drug-related crime through the Operation Anvil Garda initiative helped move Liam out of the drug dealing scene. Some of his friends had been arrested under the operation and Liam was worried that he could be next. Gangland killings in Dublin and Limerick also helped him decide to get out of the game. By now, he had been thrown out of his family home, for a third time, and he knew it was time to get serious about getting his life back in control. He went to a new treatment centre, where he decided to be more honest about his addiction and its effects. When he saw the devastation on his parents' faces as they spoke about the impact of his habit, he finally realised the pain his family had been through. The strain on them gave him the urge to pull his life together. He knew the key was moving away from the friends and acquaintances who he associated with his life as a drug user, and he decided to go to a new city. He began to attend NA meetings again and the support of other recovering addicts helped him to get control of his life. Eighteen months after his last fix, Liam now has a better life with a job, his own car, and a house he is able to rent on his own.

For him, the biggest step forward is an improvement in his relationship with his family. He says: 'They are now talking to me again. My brother has a child and he asked me to be the godfather – something I wouldn't expect.'

* * *

Liam's experience has been echoed hundreds of times in homes throughout Ireland in recent years. In some homes, there is a void which no amount of treatment or counselling can ever fill. That is because drugs like cocaine and heroin have led to the sudden and untimely deaths of young men and women throughout the country. As an investigation was underway in to the massive cocaine seizure off the Cork coast in July 2007, smaller consignments of the drug were being distributed by dealers to users in every village, town and city. However, the good times associated with cocaine use were headed towards a major public relations disaster.

When fifteen people were rushed to hospital in Waterford in the early hours of 25 November after ingesting damp cocaine at a party, it served as a health warning about the dangers of the drug. The deaths of two of them – twenty-three-year-old John Grey and cancer survivor Kevin Doyle – after several days in intensive care in Waterford Regional Hospital shocked the nation. For parents, this was a wake up call. It meant that they could not guarantee seeing their child return perfectly healthy after a night out. For young people, it was an indicator that life could easily be lost in the search for a high.

In a move which highlighted how the country had been gripped by the horror unfolding in Waterford, the Doyle family released a statement following twenty-one-year-old Kevin's death on 4 December. The family said the cocaine victim would always have a special place in their hearts, thoughts and prayers because of the heroic manner in which he overcame his battle with cancer. Focusing on the circumstances of his death, the statement continued: 'Kevin had a wonderful life before him. Because of his battle with illness, it was only now that he had the opportunity to show his true potential and to deliver on his undoubted ability. We sincerely hope that no family has to suffer the pain and anguish that we are going through. We would earnestly ask all those – both young and old – who may be tempted to dabble in potentially lethal substances to simply say no.' The statement poignantly added: 'No amount of so-called fun is worth the loss of life that so often befalls young people in Ireland today.'

His older brother, Eric, used Kevin's funeral as a medium to appeal to other young people not to play with death by using drugs. In his eulogy, he said: 'I think it's fair to say that all young people have the attitude that 'it will never happen to me'. Those who attended that party on that fateful night did not think it would happen to them. Our family didn't think it would happen to us and Kevin, above all, did not believe it was going to happen to him. If there's one message today, it's that it can and will happen to you, to me, to anybody who takes chances with drugs. Don't do it. It's not worth the risk. Say no.'

As the family of Kevin Doyle struggled to accept his death, John Grey's loved ones gathered around his bedside to say goodbye to him four days later. By now, two communities were in mourning for three young people, whose deaths had become linked to drugs. Well-known model Katy French had died in the arms of her sister two days before John Grey. She had been lying in a coma in hospital in Navan for four days. She had been taken to hospital after collapsing at a friend's house in County Meath. Toxicology results revealed a presence of cocaine in her system. Just days before she collapsed, she had celebrated her twenty-fourth birthday in Dublin with an elaborate party attended by family, friends and celebrities. Gardaí set up an investigation after her death, resulting in the arrests of four people in Meath the following February. Files were sent to the DPP after the four were released without charge.

Proof that drug-related deaths were becoming part of the 'new' Ireland was evident with the opening of a remembrance garden for victims in Carlow, the day before Mr Grey's death. The Minister in charge of Ireland's drug strategy, Pat Carey, opened the garden, which is located in Merchant's Quay Ireland's St Francis Farm residential treatment centre in Tullow. Speaking at the opening of the garden, Merchant's Quay director Tony Geoghegan said: 'Every day we seem to hear of yet another young person dying as a result of drug use. The tragic loss of a brother or sister, son or daughter, at a time when you should be full of hope for their future is devastating for families.'

There is currently no centralised database of deaths linked to drug use in Ireland. Neither is there a streamlined way of identifying how many drug-related cases come through emergency departments in Irish hospitals. Attempts were being made in 2008 by the Health Research Bureau to remedy the void in information in relation to such deaths. However, good indicators of the effects of drugs on individuals were harrowing inquests held throughout the country in 2007 and 2008. Statistics from the Dublin City Coroner, Dr Brian Farrell, revealed that 87 of the 561 inquests heard in his court in 2007 were drug-related. Of those, fourteen were connected to cocaine, while a further fourteen were directly related to heroin. Methadone was found to be directly responsible for twelve deaths, which came before the court. In the first three months of 2008, Dublin's City and County Coroners' Courts heard more than forty drug-related inquests, mostly referring to deaths which took place in 2007. Among them was the inquest of twenty-four-year-old Marie Fallon from Ballymun in Dublin. She had ingested damp cocaine on 6 June 2006. She suffered seizures and was rushed to hospital. Marie suffered a number of heart attacks and died of multi-organ failure. The coroner, Dr Brian Farrell, said her death was caused by a toxic reaction to cocaine. Warning of the dangers of cocaine use, Dr Farrell said: 'Cocaine is an unpredictable drug in its effects and its toxic effects are not dose related. I'm sorry to say this was a toxic reaction to cocaine.'

On one day at Dublin County Coroner's Court in June 2007, Dr Kieran Geraghty dealt with five cocaine-related inquests. He warned: 'Cocaine can be fatal in very small doses. You don't have to take very much of it and it can cause death the first time you use it. It can cause sudden death. The public need to be aware of this.' Six months later, he again warned of the dangers of the drug, saying it is the biggest killer among all illegal substances. Of the forty-seven drug-related deaths heard in his court in 2007, twenty-six were cocaine-related. Dr Geraghty revealed: 'Of the twenty-six cocaine-related inquests, cocaine toxicity on its own accounted for fifteen deaths, while cocaine together with heroin accounted for a further six deaths.' He added: 'I hope at least some people will pay attention to those facts and avoid drugs and avoid the company of people who use drugs. Looking back on 2007 there has been a large number of inquests into drug-related deaths. And nearly all of the deaths involved young people. In 2007, I opened seven inquests into deaths where people were shot to death, and five where they were stabbed to death, and some of these involved a drug connection.'

Coroners are not alone in seeing the effects of drug abuse at first hand. Consultant Dr Chris Luke has worked in the Mercy University Hospital and the University Hospital in Cork for almost a decade. He has regularly spoken out about the rise of drug use in Irish society. He has appeared on the *Late Late Show* on RTÉ and been interviewed in the main daily Irish newspapers. He said one of the main reasons why drug users arrive into hospitals is because of what he terms 'chaotic delirious behaviour' from a party, niteclub or a police station cell. According to Dr Luke, such admissions are regularly associated with injury and violence. He said: 'Personally, I have encountered cases involving mainly young men (but by no means exclusively men) with a bleeding nose, bitten off at a party; chest pain; several seizures, and cases of chronic polysubstance misuse.' For people working in the frontline with cocaine and heroin users, there is the added factor of aggression. He said extreme aggression is a typical condition of cocaine cases. According to the Cork-based consultant, patients who present when 'out of their heads' on these drugs are typically agitated, slow to comply with orders from staff and can, on occasion, be carriers of hepatitis B or C.

Dr Luke has also seen psychiatric cases relating to drug use, as well as homicide cases in which he strongly suspected cocaine was a trigger. Other typical reasons why drug users attend emergency departments include sudden cardiac arrests, stroke and chest pain. According to Dr Luke, chest pains in these cases are caused by a variety of complications associated with use of cocaine, ranging from accelerated coronary disease to collapsed lungs, to burned airways.

Despite the health concerns posed by the use of illegal drugs, a major survey of pubs, clubs and other social outlets across the country in December 2007 revealed a presence of cocaine in 92 per cent of the surveyed locations. Bathrooms in 269 venues were tested for the RTÉ1 *Primetime* survey, with high-profile venues including the Rose of Tralee dome, RTÉ, Croke Park and Galway Races. Panic gripped the country that Ireland was in the clutches of a cocaine epidemic.

The stark reality is that users of 'clean' drugs like cocaine fail to see a link between their recreational habit and violent crimes including gangland murders. Limerick Independent councillor, John Gilligan, agrees, having seen at first hand the damage drug-related crime can do in areas like Limerick. He said: 'Drugs are no longer just a problem for wayward kids in disadvantaged areas – use of them is affecting all sectors of society. The consumer base is huge and there seems to be a disconnect between the white collar users and the people pulling the strings in the drug deal. The people out there murdering in gangland are those who give white collar people the drugs for their weekend parties.'

The rise in the Irish economy from the mid-1990s helped provide young professionals with more disposable income, making it easy for them to turn to cocaine as a recreational drug. Clinical director of Dublin's Rutland Centre, Stephen Rowen, feels that the economic prosperity came at a good time for drug cartels in South America, who were being hit by a decrease in the market for cocaine in the US. He believes the cocaine problem in Ireland and other parts of Europe erupted after a peak in the drug's popularity in the US in the mid-1980s. He points out that the decrease in use in the US occurred as huge quantities of the drug were still being produced in South America. He said: 'Cocaine use in the US had dropped by forty per cent by the end of the last century. If the demand for it had dramatically dropped by those customers, there was a mountain of drugs that had to be unloaded somewhere. It has found its way into Europe in a big way because of the drop in the US market and the economic boom here.' From the early 1990s, cocaine use was creeping into the Irish social culture for middle-class professionals, as the Irish economy was enjoying the rush of the Celtic Tiger. It was viewed as an elite drug because it was more expensive than heroin, but by the onset of the new millennium, its value had been reduced because of easy availability. Mr Rowen said: 'It is now in every single town and village in Ireland. Users are in every social class – people who are high flyers, people who are drug dealers, people who are in business and would never have it for other than personal use.'

The Irish love affair with cocaine was reflected in a report on its use by the National Advisory Committee on Drugs (NACD) published in 2007. According to the report, cocaine use represente a larger share of the total treatment-seeking population in Ireland than ever before. The report said that the numbers presenting for cocaine treatment since the early 1990s had increased almost every year. Figures supplied to the NACD by the Drug Treatment Centre Board for the report paint a stark picture. In 1998 just 580 clients attending addiction centres run by the health boards in Ireland tested positive for cocaine use. This steadily climbed over the next seven years, to 2,330 in 2005. The typical age group for clients presenting for treatment was between twenty-five and twenty-nine years old, with two thirds of those being male.

The increase in people presenting for treatment is echoed by the increasing number of users arriving into hospital emergency departments. Dr Luke said that hospitals in Dublin's inner city have been seeing users in A&E departments since the 1980s, when heroin use in particular ravaged areas of the city centre. With the growth of the Celtic Tiger, in the mid-1990s, cocaine use began to emerge throughout the country, impacting on emergency departments from then on. Dr Luke arrived back in Ireland to work in Cork in 1999. He had been working in emergency medicine in Liverpool, and earlier in Glasgow, during the so-called 'Trainspotting era' of heroin use. He had worked at the coalface of drug addiction in the UK where, he said, usage had become a major challenge in Liverpool from the mid-1990s. Now, he typically sees a number of patients per week, who are brought to hospital for drug-associated problems, including an average of one heroin case per week. This compares with just one a year in Cork when he started working there in 1999.

Jesuit priest Fr Peter McVerry has worked with homeless

young people in Dublin for more than thirty years. From experience in shelters in the capital city, Fr McVerry said the use of drugs by people in their early twenties is very evident. However, he said the problem can start much earlier in life, as happened in Liam's case. Fr McVerry has seen situations where combinations of alcohol and cocaine made users aggressive and paranoid. Alcohol has always been the main substance abused by addicts in Ireland. However, a growing proportion are now presenting at treatment centres with combined addictions to alcohol and cocaine, a lethal cocktail. When taken together, the two come together in a user's system to form another drug called cocaethylene, a more toxic drug than either of the other two on their own. Cocaethylene is believed to present a high risk of suicidal behaviour among drug abusers.

The typical age for addicts receiving treatment at the Rutland Centre for cocaine and alcohol misuse is within the twenty-five–thirty-eight age group. The centre has 225 clients a year for alcohol, drug addictions, gambling addictions, and eating disorders. Of those, about fifty have had what Mr Rowen termed a 'destructive relationship' with cocaine. He believes that the experience of users, who can use cocaine without experiencing any health or addiction difficulties tempt other people to use it. He said: 'They tell their friends it is a great drug which gives a better sexual drive and self confidence. Those mates are not going to listen to the concerns in the media – they will follow their friends' leadership. Only one of their group may get into trouble with cocaine use while those who don't become a positive advertisement for the drug. It does not carry the same desperate stigma as other drugs. Feelings of low self esteem evaporate with use of cocaine and it makes people feel great. Using it is not just about boredom and loneliness – users want the drama and like the rollercoaster feeling.'

In his role as Governor of Mountjoy Prison in Dublin, John Lonergan has seen, first hand, the social problems associated with drug use. He is a regular speaker to communities about such effects. He questions why young people in Ireland feel they need to use a mood-altering drug in order to enjoy themselves and believes that there is confusion among that generation about how contentment can be attained.

Drug use can result in difficult experiences in the home for families of addicts, with mood swings and erratic behaviour leading to marital pressures. In extreme cases, it has led to family breakdown and homelessness for the user. Mr Rowen said: 'For every addict, there are at least four other people around them affected. These people have feelings of powerlessness and worry about finance.'

Liam's story is proof that those who develop addiction to drugs, like cocaine and heroin, are often led into a pattern of debt and despair in order to pay for their next fix. Similarly, Mr Rowen has come across situations where addicts can spend up to €1,000 in one weekend on drugs. He has also seen users, like Liam, become dealers themselves to help fund their habit. First-time users quickly move from non-criminal back-grounds to situations where they are purchasing drugs from dealers in an underworld they never thought they would be in.

As heroin use began to creep into towns and cities from 2006, a rise in crime by heroin addicts was feared. Cities like Cork and Limerick started to show signs of use of the drug. Although the amount of seizures were small in comparison with cocaine hauls, Gardaí and community leaders were con-cerned by evidence that heroin users were moving from smok-ing the lethal drug to injecting it. Two seizures, worth €200,000 each, within weeks of each other in Cork city and in West Cork, in the latter half of 2007, showed that the demand for the drug in the Cork area was getting bigger. Until then, the largest seizure had been worth a tenth of that figure. At the pre-liminary meeting of Cork city's Joint Policing Committee in December 2007, Chief Superintendent Kevin Ludlow warned that an increased use of the drug in the city would lead to a rise in criminality. Quoted in the *Evening Echo*, he said: 'Addicts have been involved in robberies here in recent months and addicts have also been arrested for shoplifting.'

Because cocaine is typically seen as the drug of the middle

classes, it is hardly surprising that its use is viewed as cleaner and less stigmatic than heroin. The common perception is that users do not have to steal to meet their needs, although Liam's story shows that some users do not have the money to fund a regular cocaine fix.

For addicts who cannot meet their debts, alternatives are regularly presented to them by their dealers. In some cases, they are forced to carry out favours, such as, carrying or storing drugs or weapons for the dealers, which can in turn lead to jail sentences. In some cases, female and male addicts turn to street prostitution to raise funds for their habits. Mules caught at airports and ports throughout the world are regularly enlisted for such jobs because of debts they have accrued with people who deal drugs.

When heroin ravaged Dublin in the 1980s, Ireland was repulsed by the dangers it posed. As well as leading to an increase in crime, use of the drug has been associated with the spread of diseases like HIV and hepatitis C because of intravenous use. Overdosing is another fatal outcome associated with heroin misuse. Dr Luke believes that cocaine poses a greater threat to society, however, particularly as he expects the epidemic to take between five and ten years more to peak. He explains: 'I feel it is premature to compare the two, since we have had a heroin problem for decades in these islands, but only recently have we seen cocaine take hold; on balance, I believe that cocaine is a greater threat to society because of the violence it engenders and the abrupt deaths it causes. Heroin and social pathology seem to be more slow burning; dozens die each year in affected communities and there is terrible petty crime and social vagrancy.' He added: 'In short, heroin is a grim reaper, but cocaine is a diabolical cyclone.'

Governor Lonergan points out that people who become addicted to drugs become immersed in a world of crime and violence that they may have not seen before. He said: 'The reality is that addicts have no choice – they become caught up in this world. As they become addicts, they are likely to see people being shot before their very eyes.'

The increasing availability of drugs and the rise in gun crime, particularly in Dublin, sparked the introduction of what had been hailed as tough legislation in May 2007 by the then Minister for Justice, Michael McDowell. The legislation strengthened bail laws, and laid out clearer guidelines for the imposing of mandatory minimum sentences for firearms and drug trafficking offences. McDowell, also a former Attorney General, had criticised the judiciary in the run up to the new anti-crime legislation package for failing too often to apply the mandatory sentence of ten years to offenders caught with more than €13,000 of drugs.

The legislation came two years after the introduction of the special operation codenamed 'Anvil', which was initially set up in Dublin to target gangland criminals. It was extended to the rest of the country in late 2006. In March 2008, then Garda Commissioner, Fachtna Murphy, said the operation had led to 570 guns being seized, 5,000 arrests being made and the recovery of €13 million worth of property since it was set up.

However, the apparent success of Anvil did little to frighten gangland figures battling for turf in their drug empires. The 2007 legislation followed the moral outrage sparked by the shooting of apprentice plumber Anthony Campbell, along with gangland figure Martin 'Marlo' Hyland in a house in Finglas, two weeks before Christmas 2006. Their deaths were among twenty-six gun murders in Ireland that year. Anthony Campbell had been working in the house where Hyland was staying, after he had been advised by Gardaí that there was a threat to his life. The fact that twenty-year-old Campbell was in the wrong place at the wrong time, brought it home to people that gun crime could come to anyone's door. That incident, and the shooting of Latvian mum Baiba Saulite, as she stood smoking a cigarette in the doorway of her home, just weeks before, marked a big turning point in the psyche of the Irish people.

In Limerick, violence during the first quarter of 2008 was testament to an in-built hatred between rival groups in that city, where a gangland feud had claimed ten lives since it began in 2000. The cycle of violence came after a split emerged between rival gangs including John and Eddie Ryan, and Christy and Kieran Keane, who had been involved in the city's lucrative drugs trade together. Enmity between the two sides since then has led to numerous gun attacks on people and houses in the affected areas of Southill, Moyross and Ballinacurra Weston. When the body of twenty-year-old James Cronin, from Janesboro, was found in a shallow grave, not far from his neighbourhood on 7 April 2008, it brought national media attention back on the Treaty City. His body was found just two days after the murder of Mark Moloney, who was shot in broad daylight, as he talked to another man outside a shop in Garryowen. The dead man had not been involved in the feud himself, but had been friendly with members of one of the factions and killed by the other side. Gardaí investigating his shooting were searching for weapons when they found James Cronin's body. Gardaí seized 150 firearms in the city, in the preceding two years, and more than 600 searches were carried out by them in the same period. In follow-up searches during the investigation into Cronin's death, officers found 30,000 ecstasy tablets stashed in a field. It came on top of seizures of up to €1 million worth of drugs in Limerick during the three weeks before the April 2008 killings.

Those attacks highlighted the involvement of teenagers in the dispute that had started with the more seasoned men like

Eddie and John Ryan, and Christy and Kieran Keane. A teenager, Stephen O'Sullivan, was charged with the murder of Mark Moloney. The two murders came on top of the arrest of a fourteen-year-old boy in the city for possession of a gun, just days before. When he came before the district court on the firearms charge, Judge Tom O'Donnell said: 'Whatever about his physical size, his streetwise attitude is stunning.' With such young figures now involved in the gangland feud, Gardaí and community leaders were united in feeling that the situation in the city had moved to a new level, as the hatred between the factions seeped down the generations and outside to friends and associates of the main players. During a press briefing after the Cronin and Moloney killings, Chief Superintendent Willie Keane said: 'Some commentators have put the feud in Limerick down to drugs and turf war and that element is there, but it is deeper than that. It is about hatred, and family hatred and this overwhelming desire to seek vengeance.'

Less than a month before the Limerick deaths, Labour Party leader Eamon Gilmore brought the issue of gangland crime and how it can be tackled before the Dáil. He said there had been 150 gun murders since the then Taoiseach, Bertie Ahern, took office in 1997. He said that only approximately twenty-four had been solved. In response, Mr Ahern acknowledged there were serious problems facing law enforcers in tackling gangland murders and attacks. He said: 'The difficulty is that, even when badly injured, criminals will not participate in normal surveillance and intelligence gathering. This is the case even when the individuals are known to the Garda. As we have seen recently, even seriously injured individuals who know who tried to kill them will not co-operate. That is a serious issue for the Garda which has informed me and the Minister for Justice, Equality and Law Reform, Deputy Brian Lenihan, that it has the legal powers but cannot force people to do so, that it can only continue its legal surveillance intelligence activity and question people to try to get this information. This is a serious problem for Gardaí; they know the gangs, on which they have good intelligence, but where there are crimes between gangs, their *modus operandi* is not to speak.' He added that this problem was mainly confined to Dublin. He said €20 million in funding was allocated to operation Anvil for 2008. Admitting that the operation will not solve the unsolved murders of the past, he said the funding would help prevent others in the future. However, in the wake of such promises, the situation in Limerick appeared to spiral out of control, prompting the nation towards, yet another, moral panic about the rise in gun crime. Ironically, despite the media-hyped murders in vicious feuds between gangs in Dublin in 2007, the number of gun-related murders in Ireland had dropped from twenty-six in 2006 to eighteen in 2007.

The majority of Irish people have no links to gangland and have no experience of such horrific killings as those in Dublin and Limerick. However, a growing number of parents are losing their children to the drugs pedalled by those involved in the gangland scene. With high-profile inquests, like those of Katy French, John Grey and Kevin Doyle, yet to be heard in 2008, it was likely that deaths linked to cocaine use would continue to dominate the headlines.

According to Dr Chris Luke, the growth in the number of such deaths in Ireland was likely to continue. He says death and destruction from drug abuse is evident everywhere, including apparent anarchy on streets, and in schools, hospitals, niteclubs, police stations, airports, train stations . . . wherever people gather. He warned: 'There's no end, other than financial ruin, death and destruction, and the very occasional lucky escape.'

NOTE: Liam not his real name

CONCLUSION

As families in Ireland struggle with their grief, the international drug traffickers, whose wares ruins the lives of so many, are busy reaping the profits of a highly lucrative industry. Prisons throughout the world are homes to couriers, who were either seduced or forced into the drug trafficking trade. But as the dust settled on the investigation files on the Dunlough Bay case, Gardaí, customs and naval officers all knew that international drugs traffickers were busy organising other shipments of cocaine, cannabis and heroin for the insatiable habits of European drug users.

There was an increase of almost 20 per cent in detections made by Gardaí in 2007 for drug dealing. In bald terms, this was an increase of 595 cases.

There was no major maritime seizure between the *Posidionia* in 1999 and the cocaine found off Mizen Head in 2007. But it is accepted that other large shipments managed to get into Ireland during that period – without being detected. It is estimated that only a tenth of illegal substances coming through the coast are discovered by law enforcement agencies.

Indeed, it is suspected that at least one large seizure was landed on the West Cork coast during the summer of 2006. Officers in the customs, navy and Gardaí readily admit that the 2007 consignment was only caught because of severe weather conditions, and the mistake of putting diesel into a petrol engine. It is likely that several consignments made it onto Irish shores without being detected in the years since 1999.

Given the increased demand for drugs, including cocaine, in the last two decades, it is not surprising that shipments grew significantly in size over that period. Until 2007, the 599kg of cocaine found in 1996 on board the *Sea Mist* was heralded as the largest ever seizure of the drug in Ireland. The €440 million haul from Dunlough Bay surpassed any consignment that had come into Ireland before 2007.

The law enforcement agencies in Ireland have combined to form the Joint Drugs Taskforce, in recent years, to tackle drug smuggling. The Maritime Analysis and Operation Centre-Narcotics (MAOC-N) in Lisbon was established in 2007 with the aim of promoting co-operation on developing intelligence on drug trafficking.

However, as the cases in *Nothing to Declare* highlight, the majority of coastal shipments are detected because of weather conditions or problems with the vessels carrying the consignments. Although intelligence has led to seizures, such as, that of the *Brime*, there was nothing to suggest that a consignment as large as that found in Dunlough Bay, in July 2007, was on its way across the Atlantic towards Ireland. If the rib had not run into trouble, the €440 million of cocaine would have not gone undetected.

PAST SEIZURES

July 1991: 700kg of cannabis resin found on the *Karma of the East* in Courtmacsherry, County Cork

December 1992: 50kg of cannabis resin thrown overboard from vessel in Cork harbour

May 1993: 150kg of cannabis resin found buried on Warren beach in Rosscarbery, after a yacht, called the *Happy Girl*, was spotted in an unusual anchorage off the coast of Cork

June 1993: 700kg of cannabis resin found on the *Tangle Wind* yacht, on a beach in Tragumna, County Cork

July 1993: 2 tonnes of cannabis resin found on a yacht called the *Brime*, off Loop Head, County Clare

November and December 1993: 1,259kg of cannabis resin trawled south of Kinsale, County Cork

August 1994: 600kg of cannabis resin found on a yacht, called the *Nicoletta*, in Ballyconneelly, County Galway

November 1994: 26kg of cannabis resin trawled off the coast of Cork

December 1994: 26.8kg of cannabis resin trawled off the coast of Cork

March 1995: 20kg of cocaine washed up at Fanore, County Clare

September and October 1995: 300kg of cannabis resin trawled from the seabed off Wexford

May 1996: 76kg of cannabis resin trawled off the coast of Cork

August 1996: 50kg of cocaine seized on board the *MV Front Guider*, in Moneypoint, County Clare

September 1996: 599kg of cocaine taken off the Sea Mist in Cobh, County Cork

November 1996: 1.7 tonnes of cannabis resin seized from a cabin cruiser, called *Plongeur Wisky*, in Kilrush, County Clare

September 1998: 320kg of cocaine found on the *Gemeos* catamaran, in Kinsale, County Cork

November 1999: 1.5 tonnes of cannabis resin on board the *Posidonia*, 10 kilometres off the Fastnet Rock, County Cork

July 2007: 1.5 tonnes of cocaine found in the waters of Dunlough Bay, off the coast of Cork, after a rib overturned

THE WRIGHT GANG

Brian Brendan Wright:
Conspiracy to evade the prohibition and importation of a controlled drugs imposed by Section 170 (2) of the Customs and Excise Management Act 1997, contrary to Section 1 (1) of the Criminal Law Act 1977; and
Conspiracy to supply drugs, contrary to Section 1 (1) of the Criminal Law Act 1977.

Ronald Soares - Count 1a, 1b

Ian Kiernan - Count 1a, 1b

Paul Rodgers - Count 1b, 1c

Brian Anthony Wright - Count 1a

Paul Shannon - Count 2c

Liliana Uribe - Count 3 (Pleaded guilty)

Kevin Hanley - Count 1a, b, c, 2a, b, c (Pleaded guilty)

Barry Fennell - Count 1c (Pleaded guilty)

Roger Newton - Count 5 (Pleaded guilty)

Hilton Van Staden - Count 1c (Pleaded guilty)

John Ewart (aka Gordon Richards) - possession of cocaine for sale or supply to others

Godfried Hoppenbrouwers - US Offences

Judith Parks - US Offences

Jim Goodrich - US Offences

Alain Deland - US Offences

Alex de Cubas - US Offences

Anni Rowland - Count 2c & 3 (Pleaded guilty)

Brian Coldwell - Count 3 (Pleaded guilty)

Gary Mace - Count 3 (Pleaded guilty)

Explanatory note on counts:

1a = 1996 importation
1b = 1997 importation
1c =1998/99 importation
2a = 1996 Conspiracy to supply
2b = 1997 Conspiracy to supply
2c = 1998/99 Conspiracy to supply
3 = Money laundering
5 = Possession with intent to supply

BIBLIOGRAPHY

Books: Bradley, Graham with Taylor, Steve, *The Wayward Lad – the Autobiography of Graham Bradley,* Great Britain (Greenwater Publishing, 2000)

Moore, Chris, *The Bankrupt, the Conman, the Mafia and the Irish Connection,* Dublin (Gill & Macmillan, 2003)

Williams, Paul, *The Untouchables – Ireland's Criminal Assets Bureau and its War on Organised Crime,* Dublin (Merlin Publishing, 2006)

Reports: Revenue, *Annual Report 2007*
Revenue, *Annual Report 2006*
Garda Síochana, *Annual Report 2006*
World Customs Organisation, *Customs and Drug Report 2006*
United Nations Office on Drugs and Crime, *World Drug Report 2007*
United States Department of State, *International Narcotics Control Strategy Report 2008*
National Advisory Committee on Drugs, *An Overview of Cocaine Use in Ireland II,* 2007
National Advisory Committee on Drugs *Drug Use in Ireland and Northern Ireland: First Results from the*

2006/2007 Drug Prevalence Strategy

Media: *Evening Echo, Irish Examiner* and *Cork Examiner, The Irish Times* and *Sunday Times, Irish Independent* and *Sunday Independent, Sunday Tribune, Sunday Times* (South Africa), *The Times, Sunday Business Post, Sunday World, Irish Daily Mirror, Irish Daily Star, Daily Mail, The Guardian, Daily Telegraph, The Independent, Irish News, Belfast Telegraph, Southern Star, The Sun, Watford Observer, Miami Herald, Los Angeles Times,* BBC, RTÉ and TV3.

Internet: http://historical-debates.oireachtas.ie
www.modernghana.com
www.ndc.hrb.ie